A Team M

M000100247

Doug Pederson and the Philadelphia Eagles' Journey to the Super Bowl

By **Turron Davenport**

A Team Makes a Miracle:
Doug Pederson and the Philadelphia Eagles'
Journey to the Super Bowl

Published by Blue River Press
Indianapolis, Indiana
www.brpressbooks.com

Distributed by Cardinal Publishers Group
317-352-8200 phone
317-352-8202 fax
www.cardinalpub.com

ISBN: 978-1-68157-149-2

Cover Design: David Miles
Book Design: Dave Reed
Cover Photo: AP Images
Editor: Dani McCormick

Printed in the United States of America

10 9 8 7 6 5 4 3 2 1   18 19 20 21 22 23 24 25 26 27

Contents

Introduction

There were plenty of thoughts that went through Eagles head coach Doug Pederson's mind as he approached the podium the morning after taking down the mighty Patriots in Super Bowl LII. Pederson had done what no other Philadelphia football coach was able to do in the modern era. He led an Eagles team that brought the city their first Lombardi Trophy.

In only two years, Pederson went from what critics considered to be a questionable hire by the Eagles to the top of the NFL. Pederson's rise was rapid and well calculated.

He did things his way, even when his style was viewed as the wrong way to do things. As a result, Pederson has cemented himself as a Philadelphia sports icon.

Pederson wasn't the only one to defeat the odds en route to becoming a Super Bowl champion. There were many others on the Eagles that did so as well.

Foreword

Just a few days after the Eagles relieved Chip Kelly of his duties as head coach; I received an email from a reader who suggested Doug Pederson as their next head coach.

I didn't laugh out loud, but I smiled and quickly replied I didn't think that was a strong possibility. Pederson's lack of experience (he had only worked for Andy Reid), and what appeared to be a wealth of other candidates were reasons for my skepticism.

Boy was I wrong. Well, not entirely.

The Eagles didn't really want Pederson, either.

They wanted Adam Gase and couldn't wait to get him into the NovaCare Complex. After the cursory interview with running backs coach Duce Staley to satisfy the Rooney Rule requirement, Gase flew to Philadelphia.

They were the first team the then Chicago Bears offensive coordinator interviewed with. Gase was the first serious candidate the Eagles interviewed for the job.

It just wasn't love at first sight. Gase went to Miami next and quickly accepted the Dolphins head coaching position, forcing the Eagles to look elsewhere.

Then Giants offensive coordinator, Ben McAdoo was also ahead of Pederson on the Eagles' wish list. There was a welcome basket prepared and ready for him when he was scheduled for his second interview with the team. The Giants intercepted it, like a wayward Eli Manning pass and kept McAdoo in New Jersey as their head coach.

To this day, I am not sure what the story was with Tom Coughlin. But, I was pretty sure then and even more sure now he was never going to be the Eagles head coach.

That would be Pederson, as my astute emailer quickly predicted.

Pederson's first, of what will likely be many years as head coach of the Eagles, was my last of, many years (32 to be exact), covering the team.

I am not going to sit here with 20-20 hindsight and tell you I knew he was going to win a Super Bowl in his second year, or even his third, fourth of fifth year.

I will tell you this though.

Pederson, in that first year, impressed me. If you read anything of mine over the past 32 years, you know I was never afraid to criticize a coach or his decisions, be it Rich Kotite, Ray Rhodes, or especially Andy Reid.

Pederson would be next. And this would be all too easy. Except it wasn't.

If nothing else that first year Pederson was extremely likable and accessible. That does not excuse him from criticism by any means, but if he's willing to explain why he did what he did and do it in a pleasant manner, well it sure beats "I have to do a better job..."

Pederson showed crazy aggressiveness that first year. The kind of stuff fans thought they were going to get with Kelly, but never really did.

He went for it on fourth down against the odds, went for two-point conversions more than any other team. Even did it down one late in the fourth quarter at Baltimore.

A lot of that against-the-norm coaching didn't work his first year, because the team just wasn't quite good enough to make it work.

Once Pederson had better players, on both sides of the ball, those risk-taking calls made him look like a genius. And it did the same for that guy who sent me the email back at the end of 2015.

—Mark Eckel, *Trenton Times* and *NJ.com* Eagles reporter

A Team Makes a Miracle

Doug Pederson

Building As a Backup

Doug Pederson bounced around when he first got into professional football, spending most of his career as a backup quarterback in the NFL. It was these humble beginnings that molded him into the coach he is today.

His journey began when he signed with the Miami Dolphins as a rookie free agent out of Northeast Louisiana University (now the University of Louisiana at Monroe). The Dolphins waived Pederson before the regular season began.

After spending the 1991 season as a free agent, Pederson was still looking to play football. An opportunity arose when the New York/New Jersey Knights of the World League of American Football selected him in the fifth round for the first pool of draft-eligible players in February 1992. Pederson was the backup quarterback to Reggie Slack for the Knights from March to May 1992.

After a brief one-year stint in the World League, Pederson re-signed with the Dolphins in 1992. Pederson spent the 1992 training camp with the Dolphins, before being released during final roster cuts again. This time he was signed to the practice squad only to be released once more.

The Dolphins signed Pederson to the practice squad again in 1993, which was when his break finally came. Unfortunately, the break happened because of an injury to a future Hall of Famer. Starting quarterback Dan Marino ruptured his Achilles in a Week Six game against the Cleveland Browns.

Backup Scott Mitchell was thrust into action, and Marino was placed on injured reserve. That opened up a spot on the roster for Pederson and gave him an opportunity to be the backup quarterback.

Pederson served in the backup role for four games, making his NFL debut in a Week Eight matchup against the Indianapolis Colts. One of the highlights of Pederson's first season in the NFL ironically came against the Eagles.

Pederson entered the Week Eleven game in the third quarter after Mitchell suffered a separated shoulder. He went 3-for-6 for 34 yards and completed several crucial third downs helping head coach Don Shula win his NFL-record 325th victory as a coach.

The backup role came calling once again for Pederson when the Dolphins signed veteran Steve DeBerg to be the starter while Mitchell and Marino were out. When Mitchell came back, Pederson was released.

After re-signing with the Dolphins, Pederson spent the 1994 season as the number three quarterback behind Marino and Bernie Kosar. The Dolphins made Pederson available for the expansion draft which resulted in him being selected by the Carolina Panthers in the 22nd round in 1995.

That was where Pederson made a connection that would be rewarding during his coaching career. Pederson became friends with fellow quarterback Frank Reich before being released by the Panthers months after the expansion draft. Reich would later become Pederson's offensive coordinator when he took over as head coach of the Eagles in 2016.

Being released by the Panthers led to Pederson returning to the World League with the Rhein Fire. Another injury to Marino led to Pederson returning to the Dolphins once again in Week Six of the 1995 season only to be released for the final time when Marino returned in Week Nine.

The yo-yo-like start to Pederson's playing career helped establish the humble mindset that has allowed him to not let a Super Bowl win make him complacent. It helps give him that edge to push his guys to compete.

After the back and forth with the Dolphins, things started to settle down for Pederson. He found a home with the Green Bay Packers as Brett Favre's backup.

Pederson stuck with the Packers for four seasons including the 1996 Super Bowl champion team that he said the 2017 Eagles reminded him of talent-wise. As Brett Favre's backup, Pederson didn't get many opportunities to play because Favre didn't miss a game due to injury.

Pederson did, however, get a chance to play in a Week Five game against the Minnesota Vikings in 1998. He threw two touchdowns in mop-up duty but suffered a broken jaw that cost him the next four games.

The injury happened when Pederson was hit by Vikings cornerback Corey Fuller as he threw a touchdown pass. Despite breaking his jaw, Pederson was back on the field for the next play to be the placeholder for the point after.

"He kind of mumbled, 'Something's wrong with my jaw,' but he got the hold down, and we made the kick," Longwell said after the game. "We usually would head-butt after a PAT or a field goal, and instead he was like, 'I've got to get this thing looked at.' You could tell he was hurting. But he stayed out there and held and got the cadence out and everything. It was pretty impressive that he even shouted."

While with the Packers, it became clear that Pederson had a very cerebral approach to the game. As a backup, Pederson was another set of eyes for Favre when he came off of the field.

"Doug wanted to chart games because he felt like he was really in the game, and he was so good at getting Brett and Mike and Andy real accurate information, and he was doing it from the sideline," fellow quarterback Matt Hasselbeck said via ESPN. "I feel like I've been around a lot of great coaches. Doug was never my coach, but he probably taught me the most that first year."

Hasselbeck said Pederson was able to tell things the defensive line was doing from watching them at field level. His ability to fish out tendencies on the defensive front caused Favre to call him "The Front Doctor."

"There was one game where he discovered if the defensive end was the last guy to put his hand in the dirt, that he would be the guy fire-zoning—dropping out—so the blitz is coming away from him," Hasselbeck said.

He was also someone that other players on the other side of the ball benefited from. One of which was veteran safety LeRoy Butler.

"Doug was smart. There was only one guy that can control Brett Favre, and that was Doug Pederson. I'd get beat on a play in practice, I didn't go to talk to [defensive backs coach] Bob Valesente," Butler said on ESPN. "I went over to Doug and said, 'What was I missing on that play?' I've been dying to tell somebody this: Doug was the smartest guy I've ever had a conversation with."

Favre was more comfortable with Pederson as his backup. Having the support during the week in film study and game preparation was invaluable to Favre.

"He thought the way I thought. He knew me. He knew what I was thinking, and he was able to relay that to the coach, or the play-caller. Not a lot of the backup QBs have the headset on, but I wanted him talking to the coach," Favre told Scout.com before Super Bowl LII.

"He'd tell the play-caller, Mike [Holmgren] or Sherm [Lewis, offensive coordinator] or Mike [Sherman], 'Think check down.' Or, 'Third-and-three, expect this.' He was right so often. Some quarterbacks don't want anything in their ear but the play. I did.

"I would say, 'Make sure to give me reminders.' So he'd say, 'Hey, Merton Hanks likes to come from the weak side here,' or 'Brad Culpepper is tilted on the nose here—be careful for the weak-side blitz.' He just knew how I thought."

Some of Pederson's best moments came with the Packers. They were the team he spent the most time with as a player.

Backing up Favre was something that Pederson loved to do. However, all good things must come to an end.

First Days as an Eagle

While in Green Bay, Pederson grew close to Andy Reid. Reid was Pederson's QB coach in 1997 and 1998. Once Reid was named the head coach of the Eagles in 1999, Pederson signed a three-year, $4.5 million contract with Philadelphia allowing him to become their starting quarterback.

Reid brought Pederson along with him to Philadelphia to help install his offense and serve as a bridge for Donovan McNabb, who was selected with the number two pick in the 1999 NFL Draft. Pederson started the first nine games and posted a 2 – 7 record; a 51.6% completion rate; 1,168 passing yards; six touchdowns; and nine interceptions.

He was benched in favor of McNabb at halftime of a Week Nine game against the Carolina Panthers after going 3-of-9 for 28 yards and being down 23-0. Pederson was released by the Eagles in 2000 and signed with the Browns after considering retirement.

He signed a two-year contract with the Browns in 2000 to be the number three quarterback behind backup Spergon Wynn and starter Tim Couch. Couch was the number one pick, just ahead of McNabb in the 2000 NFL Draft.

After Couch suffered a season-ending injury in Week Seven, Pederson started the next six games, posting a 1 – 5 record. Bruised ribs caused Pederson to be knocked out of a Week Thirteen game against the Baltimore Ravens. Wynn started the next week against the Jacksonville Jaguars before suffering a season-ending injury and being replaced by Pederson.

Pederson's final two games as a Brown were losses. The Browns lost 35 – 24 to his former team, the Eagles, and were shutout 24 – 0 by the Tennessee Titans. The Browns released Pederson in 2001.

Back to the Pack

Former Packers head coach Mike Holmgren resigned from Green Bay and moved on to coach the Seattle Seahawks in 1998. The Packers traded Matt Hasselback to Holmgren and the Seahawks in 2001.

That move opened the door for Pederson to return to the Packers on a one-year contract. The deal may not have happened if it wasn't for a phone call from Hasselback to Pederson.

Hasselback and Pederson had been teammates in Green Bay in 1998. Both players had developed a close relationship with kicker Ryan Longwell.

Longwell was with the Packers from 1997 – 2005. He had two holders during his time in Green Bay, Pederson and Hasselback.

The Browns released Pederson in 2001, and he seemed to be done with football. The perils of being a journeyman had taken its toll on Pederson.

With Hasselback being traded, Longwell wanted Pederson back in Green Bay to be his placeholder, so he asked Hasselback to reach out to him.

"Doug had just had a couple of really tough years in Philly and then in Cleveland, and I think he was done with the NFL," Hasselback told ESPN. "He was beaten down and somewhat broken, and he was done with football, and he was going home. I think he was going to coach high school football.

"I just remember having this conversation, and he was saying, 'You don't know what this year was like,'" Hasselbeck said. "I told him, 'Come here, hold for Ryan, back up Brett and play in four preseason games.'"

Those four preseason games turned into four years. Pederson was the primary backup for all of 2001 and added placeholder duties as well that year.

Being back with Favre rejuvenated Pederson.

The Packers once again signed Pederson to a one-year deal. This one was worth $650,000. Pederson resumed the same role as backup and placeholder, but he finally saw game action in relief of Favre in 2002.

Favre suffered a sprained knee in a Week Seven game against the Washington Redskins. Pederson took over in the second half and went 9-for-15 for 78 yards to help win the game 30 – 9. Pederson also played in games against the Miami Dolphins, Detroit Lions, and New York Jets.

After ending the season with 19 completions on 28 pass attempts for 134 yards and one touchdown pass, Pederson once again re-signed with the Packers.

Head coach Mike Sherman seemed to be pleased with Pederson as the backup. The deal was another one-year contract but increased to $750,000 and kept him with the team in 2003.

Favre's father passed away in 2003. Pederson was with Favre when he got the news. In fact, it was Pederson who received a call from Favre's wife Deanna to explain what happened.

Soon after the news, the Packers had to travel to Oakland to face the Raiders. Favre had butterflies before the game because he wanted to honor his father with a stellar outing. Pederson served as a calming influence for Favre during pregame warmups.

"Doug stayed by my side," Favre told ESPN. "Finally he says to me, 'Let's go out and throw, kid.' So we went out on the field, me and him. I'm bouncing it, throwing it over his head. I could not throw a ten-yard pass. I'm getting ready to play on 'Monday Night Football.' I'm nervous; I'm just out of it. I am going to make a fool of myself in this game."

Favre wasn't known as a religious person, but Pederson had no hesitation approaching him and saying a prayer.

"We go back inside. I'm shaken up. Doug comes to my locker. He says, 'It's gonna be okay.' He said a prayer, right there. He put his hands on my shoulder, said a prayer. Then he bumps his fists real lightly on my shoulder. He tells me, 'You're gonna be great tonight. You're gonna play an awesome game.'"

Favre completed 22 of 30 pass attempts for 399 yards and four touchdowns against the Raiders that night. As Pederson told him before the game, Favre played awesomely.

This is an example of Pederson's willingness to incorporate faith into the equation. Faith allowed Pederson to be confident in Favre's ability to go out and have an outstanding showing. That same faith is something that permeates through the Eagles' locker room.

Pederson signed another one-year deal with the Packers in 2004. This time the team brought in competition for the backup spot. Former number one pick Tim Couch was signed to compete with Pederson.

The two had been teammates back in Cleveland. Pederson fought off Couch and won the job. In a Week Three game against the Indianapolis Colts, Pederson replaced Favre in a blowout loss and went 4-of-6 for 34 yards and an interception.

The next week against the New York Giants, Favre sustained a concussion in the third quarter, and Pederson was thrust into action again. Pederson went 7-of-17 for 86 yards and an interception in the loss before he suffered a hit to his side in the third quarter that resulted in a cracked bone in his back, a torn muscle in his side, and a broken rib.

Pederson stayed in the game up until the last snap, when he was replaced by third-string quarterback Craig Nall. After being placed on injured reserve, Pederson retired in the offseason.

It was clear that Pederson was destined to be a coach. He had unofficially been playing the role of coach to many of his teammates during his playing days.

Calvary Baptist—Introduction to Coaching

After retiring in March 2005, Pederson immediately took over as the head coach of Calvary Baptist Academy, a private Christian high school in Shreveport, Louisiana. Calvary was going into its second year as a program when Pederson signed on to be their head coach.

Coaching in high school was something that Pederson had his sights on before being talked into returning to the Packers by former teammate Matt Hasselback. It was only natural that he made the move soon after retiring.

"I always knew coaching was in my future. I just didn't know at what level. My passion and my desire are to coach high school football," Pederson told *The Shreveport Times* after he was hired as Calvary's head coach."

Having played college ball at Northeast Louisiana University from 1987 through 1990, coaching at Calvary was a homecoming of sorts. Pederson was the head coach at Calvary for four years, posting a 33 – 7 record in the regular season, and an 8 – 3 record in the post-season.

"It was my first head coaching job when I retired. Those four years were special to me because, one, my family and my boys were right there in the school with me, being a private school," Pederson said during a press conference in January. "And [then] just watching the kids grow over a four-year period and then having the chance to see some of them go on to play college football or have great careers after college.

"Not necessarily in athletics but just as students, as well. [I] had a chance to play in some playoff games and almost make it to a state championship a couple times down there. Those are special moments and moments that I'll remember."

Calvary went 5 – 6 and lost in the first round of the state playoffs in Pederson's first season. They made it to the state playoffs in each of Pederson's four seasons as head coach. In 2007, Pederson led the Calvary to the semifinals and to their first district title.

One of the first tests for Pederson at Calvary came a year after he accepted the position as head coach of the program. He led Calvary to the Class 2A Louisiana State semifinals.

They went against Louisiana powerhouse Milan High led by head coach Rich Gaille. Milan cruised to a 35 – 14 win and advanced to the championship game. Even though Gaille's team dealt Pederson's squad a 21-point loss, Gaille was impressed with Pederson.

"Doug wanted to find out whether he wanted to coach or not," Gaille told the *Philadelphia Inquirer* in January of 2018. "And, to his credit, instead of calling in a favor with somebody in the NFL, he took the job at Calvary Baptist. He was in on the ground floor, and he found out what coaching was all about.

"That says something. At this level, if there's a grass field that's not marked, guess who has to do it? The uniforms have to get washed by someone after the game. Doug discovered in his time at Calvary that this was something he really wanted to do."

Gaille expanded on his compliment of Pederson, taking it from the football field to him as a person. "You've gotta love somebody who will get in there with teenagers and spend all day with them, as goofy as teenagers are. Doug's got class, he cares about people, and it's evident that he does. That's not a false notion. Nothing is too big or too small for him to be able to engage in. He has a very good sense of what is important and what isn't important."

For Pederson, spending time with the kids, helping launch them to success later in life helped him find inner peace.

"I was extremely happy," he said. "Those were the best four years of my life. As a coach, as a mentor to young men, to high school boys. Thinking back on those four years, it taught me a bigger lesson. I wondered, *Can I teach football? Can I coach football?* Here I come from fourteen years in the National Football League as a player, soaking everything in with some great coaches, some great players, some really great offensive minds."

Despite enjoying his time with the kids at Calvary, Pederson knew he had a more significant calling. The time was coming when he had to make the decision to leave Calvary and go to the next level. His former coach Andy Reid and the NFL were waiting.

"The advice that I was getting from some of my coaches and peers was, you need to go find out if you can teach and coach. Do you like the journey? Do you like the process? Even though it was a high school, do you like putting in the time? Do you like teaching? And I did. I loved coaching. I loved teaching those kids. And it let me know this is what I wanted to do."

<u>Kicking it in Kansas City</u>

After two seasons as quarterback coach, Pederson followed Andy Reid to the Kansas City Chiefs when the Eagles decided to move on in 2013.

While in Kansas City, Pederson was given the liberty to call plays in the second half of games during his final year with the Chiefs.

"I was able to call plays, really, since the Pittsburgh game," Pederson said. "Coach Reid and I had a great understanding, a great feel for the game. He allowed me to call the second half of every football game from that Steeler game on."

Pederson said Reid gave him the opportunity to call plays as a changeup. There were times when they felt like the defensive coordinator might have had a bead on them, so Reid and Pederson presented a different twist by using a different play caller.

"It's a way to kind of view the game without having to call the play for a series or two," Pederson said during his introductory press conference as Eagles head coach. "Whether you're moving the ball or not and you get it from a different set of eyes, and he's given the faith and trust in me to do that, and we get a lot of input throughout the game anyway, and it's just sometimes a change of pace for a defensive coordinator."

As a member of the Chiefs' coaching staff, Pederson got the chance to work with Alex Smith after passing up on being his QB coach in San Francisco in 2005. Smith had played for Jim Harbaugh and offensive coordinator Greg Roman with the 49ers.

His past experience with read-option plays in college at Utah was something that Harbaugh and Roman put in play in San Francisco. That part of the offense was taken to another level when backup Colin Kaepernick took over after Smith suffered a concussion against the St. Louis Rams.

Smith was traded to the Chiefs soon after Andy Reid took over with Pederson as the offensive coordinator. One of the things the coaching staff wanted to do was take advantage of Smith's athleticism.

Smith introduced Reid and Pederson to some of the read-option concepts. This part of the offense was something that Pederson would later take with him to Philadelphia to use with Carson Wentz and Nick Foles.

"I'd say they've been around for a while. I couldn't give you a year, but for me, it was back in 2013 when Alex and I crossed paths in Kansas City," Pederson said on Thursday. "We looked at some of the things they did in San Francisco with the creative stuff offensively. That's where it took off for me personally, and now it's been a part of the offense that I've been associated with over the last four or five years."

Pederson's eyes were opened to a different way of executing plays which put more control into the quarterback's hands during the play. This would later prove to be a considerable part of Pederson's success with Carson Wentz in Philadelphia.

"It was all a new world for me. . . . It's going to continue to develop," Pederson said. "It goes hand in hand with the quick passing game. The ball gets out of the quarterback's hands, and you don't have to block everybody."

Pederson's final game with Smith came against the Patriots in the 2016 divisional playoffs. Smith threw the ball 50 times but completed 29 passes for 246 yards and one touchdown.

It was not enough, the Chiefs fell to New England by a score of 27 – 20. The season was over for the Chiefs. Soon afterward, so was Pederson's time as offensive coordinator in Kansas City.

Out of Andy's Shadow

After going 26 – 21 from 2013 – 2015 under head coach Chip Kelly, the Eagles were ready to go in a different direction. Kelly was not as endearing to the players as Reid was, even though for the most part, this was a different group.

However, there was a desire for the old school way of doing things. The franchise wanted a coach that was going to be hands-on and correct players on the field during practice rather than just in a classroom. Team owner Jeffrey Lurie also had to appoint a new chief to head the personnel department. Kelly had assumed most of the control over personnel and banished former GM Howie Roseman to a lesser role.

Lurie ceded control of team personnel to Roseman and together along with Team President Don Smolenski, they conducted a search for a new coach. Adam Gase was considered to be a strong candidate. He was fresh off of a season in which he helped guide Bears quarterback Jay Cutler to one of his better seasons in Chicago. Gase interviewed for the head coach position with the Eagles and impressed them.

However, they wanted to talk to Pederson before making the final decision. Pederson was a little busy at the time as the offensive coordinator of the Kansas City Chiefs as they prepared for the playoffs.

Gase had a few other interviews, one of which was with Miami. The Dolphins offered the head coach position to Gase, and he accepted. That left the Eagles without a coach but still waiting to interview Pederson.

While they were waiting, the Eagles interviewed former Giants offensive coordinator Ben McAdoo. They also interviewed runningback coach Duce Staley and Pat Shurmur, both of which had been on Kelly's staff.

Despite having fired Reid in 2013, the Eagles brass still had a close relationship with him. They reached out to Reid for advice about Pederson. Naturally, Reid gave a ringing endorsement.

Pederson finally sat down with the Eagles before a divisional playoff game against the New England Patriots. It was no secret that Pederson came highly recommended by Reid. That wasn't lost on Pederson when he spoke to the Kansas City media after the interview with the Eagles.

"It's been tremendous. He is a great mentor of mine. I worked for him in Philadelphia, so I understand that climate, that market, and that structure there. If it's in my future to become a head coach, there are a lot of great examples of him leading a team and organization that I can use in my future as well," Pederson said in a press conference before playing the New England Patriots in the 2016 NFL Playoffs.

Pederson's time in Green Bay helped mold his football mind. It was there that he first got introduced to the West Coast Offense that would become a staple of his later teams.

Pederson was able to learn from Reid as his QB coach and his two head coaches with the Packers, Mike Holmgren, and Mike Sherman. "I go back to my days in Green Bay with Mike Holmgren," Pederson said during a press conference before the NFC Championship against the Minnesota Vikings. "He was a little bit that way in some of his play calls, play design a little bit. And traditionally in the West Coast system, it's always been about motions and shifts and quick passing and things of that nature. That will never change in this game. It's always going to be that way.

"So Mike is definitely one of the guys. I can think back, too, on Mike Sherman, when I had him. He was probably more on the run-game side of things and could be a little creative that way in the run-game and utilizing our personnel in the run-game, as well. So a couple of those guys, really, in my days at Green Bay [were helpful]."

Pederson was named the head coach of the Eagles, but many questioned the team's decision. Some even viewed it as a move that came because they ran out of options. Although the move was met with scrutiny, one of Pederson's teammates from their days with the Packers had some positive things to say about the new head coach. "A lot of times when Doug Pederson was the backup quarterback to Brett Favre, it was Pederson talking to the wide receivers, the tight ends, and explain[ing] what was going on and what he saw. The good thing about Doug is he remained in the same system for about twenty years. He has a lot of knowledge about the West Coast offense," former Packers wide receiver Antonio Freeman said.

"There is a deep trail for this West Coast offense. Doug has been in the system for twenty years and knows the X's and O's. He knows the ins and outs so I can speak for Doug as an offensive mind. He is a phenomenal mind in the NFL. The knowledge offensively is what will be key for Doug Pederson."

Freeman pointed out how the quick-passing game with three-step drops by the quarterback was going to be something that Pederson would employ after seeing Andy Reid and Mike Holmgren use it when he played. He also referenced the personnel changes and formation switches that became a staple in the West Coast offense.

Most importantly, he tied Pederson's roots back to one of the best offensive minds ever in former 49ers head coach Bill Walsh. As a backup quarterback, Pederson got to prepare for the game like as if he was going to be the starter. However, on game day he saw the game from the perspective of a coach. That is what made Pederson so ready to take on the job of leading the Eagles.

Freeman looked at Pederson's time as a backup as an opportunity to see the game from a unique perspective. "From a backup standpoint, you are the guy that pretty much never gets a chance to play. You watch everything great about the starting quarterback," Freeman said after Pederson was named head coach. "But you also get to watch everything not so great. You get to analyze all of that so you can incorporate all of that into being a coach.

"One of the concepts that Pederson likes to use in Philadelphia is using extra tight ends. While Pederson was with the Packers, the team relied heavily on tight ends such as Bubba Franks, Mark Chmura, and both in the blocking game as well as catching passes."

"Of course, . . . we had multiple tight ends back then we used a lot and still use them today," Pederson said referring to the Packers' scheme. "We introduced the extra offensive lineman back then. That was always a little different, a unique style. So just things like that have sort of stuck with me over the years when designing either run-plays or passing schemes as we go."

When asked about the benefits of two-tight end packages after the Eagles selected South Dakota State tight end in the 2018 NFL Draft, Pederson's eyes lit up. It was clear that he was envisioning how he would be able to use Goedert and All-Pro tight end Zach Ertz on the field at the same time.

"Well, it's beneficial for a couple reasons. One, it's in the run game. You've got some bigger bodies. A lot of times you see the fullback position. It's kind of a few teams have a fullback position and they're using a second or third tight end, so it gives you the ability to run more power schemes and gap schemes and move that second tight end around a little bit and utilize him in the run game," Pederson explained.

"Then it creates match-ups. If he's an athletic guy, like a Zach Ertz, we can move him around, spread him out. He's good in space and understands spatial awareness. He's great in man coverage because he can separate at the top of the route. Those become big bodies on smaller bodies. Those are the match-ups that we try to create through game planning and through studying our opponents. That's what having two tight ends and having that twelve personnel—we call it 'tiger personnel'—on the field allows us to do. And that's what we've been able to do the first two years, and we'll continue that now with the complement of players that we have in that tight end room."

Getting the job was no easy task. Eagles owner Jeffrey Lurie desperately wanted to return to the glory days when his team was one of the most successful teams under Reid. Their only shortcoming was not winning a Super Bowl. Pederson had to convince Lurie and newly appointed Executive VP of football operations Howie Roseman that he was the man to do the unthinkable in Philadelphia. Roseman was eager to rebound from his demotion from GM status when Chip Kelly was around.

"I think one of the things that Jeffrey [Lurie] talked about that he was looking for in the interview process was emotional intelligence. He wanted someone who had that characteristic and ability to relate to people like the players, the coaches, and the whole organization," Eagles President Don Smolenski said. "I think that after the interviews that we had talking to the various candidates, then the time spent with Doug and the positive endorsement from coach Reid, as well as a little bit of history, you kind of knew what you were getting. That certainly played a role in our decision."

The pressure was on for them to find the right guy. For Pederson, the pressure was on to sell them that he was the right guy and that leading the Eagles was the best job for him. Hearing Pederson explain the offense he would install and his plan with the same passion with which he described the 'tiger package' was a selling point during the interview.

The first order on the table was figuring out what to do with the quarterback situation. When Pederson took over, Sam Bradford was a free agent, and Mark Sanchez was the other significant quarterback on the roster. Pederson wanted to know what they were going to do at quarterback. The team had the number 13 pick in the 2016 NFL Draft, which was not a place where they could expect to get a franchise quarterback.

Although his focus was on coaching, Pederson knew that figuring out the quarterback situation was going to be a collaborative effort. "If you do more with the personnel, it's going to take you away from football. It's going to take you away from football. I wanted to coach football," Pederson said when asked about having front office control and coaching. "We hire professionals to do personnel with our input as coaches. I mean, they make the final decision on players, but that is not without having extensive conversations with coaches."

Pederson's initial thoughts were to re-sign Bradford and bring in a quarterback to develop into his replacement. Bradford was in effect going to be a bridge to the next quarterback, keep the Eagles from doing a total reboot. Ironically, this was a similar situation to what Pederson was a part of when he first got to Philadelphia as a player. He was the stopgap starter until Donovan McNabb was ready to take over.

Pederson's plan made sense to the Eagles brass. But sometimes things don't always go as planned. In Philadelphia's case, that was for the better. Things played out pretty nicely thanks to a couple of trades by Roseman. The Eagles were able to get into a position to select one of the top two quarterbacks in the 2016 draft class.

One of the other selling points for Pederson was getting back to an old-school mindset and style of play. A big part of that was reintroducing the physical aspect of practice on a consistent basis. Under Chip Kelly, the Eagles had gone to more of a scientific approach. They practiced swiftly, trying to get as many plays worked through as possible. There wasn't much hitting in practice. Players were rarely practicing in full pads under Kelly. With that came the loss of physicality on game day. The Eagles' defenders were a below-average tackling team.

Pederson made it clear that wasn't going to be the case under his watch. "The fact was we were going to work hard and have a tough, physical training camp. We were going to hit and do all of the things that I knew we needed to get back to here," Pederson said. "You lose a little bit of that physicality if you aren't constantly hitting. You sell them on that and that being an offensive guy, we would focus on offense."

Pederson explained how he was going to have that same physicality on offense as well. "I got into the type of offense that we would run a little bit and just told them I would come in and work hard. They knew me; I knew them, so there wasn't a lot of explaining to do. There was a lot of familiarity with these guys. They knew me and my track record in Kansas City. It was an easy conversation," Pederson explained.

Building the Coaching Staff

Constructing a coaching staff was one of the first things that Pederson did right. He put together a group of coaches that exuded passion for football. Their love for the game resonated with them when they spoke.

The first hire was defensive coordinator Jim Schwartz. Pederson, in essence, followed the formula that led to the most success for Reid when he was in Philadelphia. Hiring a mastermind to hold down the defensive side of the ball allowed Reid to focus on getting the offense in gear. Schwartz is also a former head coach, so he was a sounding board for Pederson to bounce ideas off of as he started his career as a head coach.

Schwartz was also someone that had no problem holding players accountable. "I know when I was a head coach when I served that I wanted people around the building who were enforcing my rules, and I did that for him," Schwartz said. "I respect that position. I'm going to execute the job the way he outlined it for me. I think anything else we can't really worry about."

Schwartz pointed out an example of how he enforced Pederson's rules during a press conference in December. Pederson had a rule where players could not be in the cafeteria wearing sleeveless shirts. A player was in the cafeteria with a sleeveless shirt on, and when Schwartz saw him, he told the player to leave the cafeteria and put a shirt on before returning. That's the kind of support that a new coach who is trying to build a culture needs.

Early in the 2017 season, there were accusations that Schwartz was trying to undermine Pederson in hopes of becoming the Eagles head coach. He quickly put those thoughts to rest. "I'll say this, and I'll say this unequivocally: I am very comfortable with my relationship with Doug Pederson," Schwartz said. "And I know he's comfortable in his relationship with me."

The next decision that Pederson made regarding the coaching staff was to bring Frank Reich on as his offensive coordinator. Reich and Pederson had crossed paths back when they were in training camp together with the Carolina Panthers after the expansion draft. Reich had served as the San Diego Chargers' offensive coordinator over the previous two seasons. The Chargers fired Reich in January 2016. Pederson hired Reich just over two weeks later. Reich didn't call the plays but was a big part of installing the game plan. He and Pederson used to have long talks the Saturday night before games when they were together.

"We just kind of go back through everything one last time. And for the most part we're just kind of sitting and telling stories, just kind of reminiscing about the season, maybe the week we just had or something like that," Pederson said as he reflected on their Saturday night meetings during a press conference before the Super Bowl. "But it's just a review of the plan and make sure that we're set on whatever our openers are for that particular game, make sure we're all set and just kind of go over everything one more time."

They grew close over the time they spent together. "I'll miss the relationship we had for two years. He was the guy that I handpicked to come in and be the offensive coordinator," Pederson said soon after Reich was hired to be the head coach of the Indianapolis Colts. "He took over. He took charge of the offense. He's a great teacher. He and I collaborated on that, just the overall coordinating of the offense."

Before the 2017 NFC Championship game against the Minnesota Vikings, Reich was asked about the coaching staff that Pederson assembled. "Coach [Pederson] has literally put together the best staff that you can possibly imagine and that's how we work. We work as a staff together. It's fun to do it that way," Reich said.

He praised Pederson for giving the other coaches the opportunity to have input on the game plan and preparation. "It's fun when we've got a head coach who shares that responsibility. . . . As the role of offensive coordinator, that's what you do: you coordinate," Reich explained. "You take all the great resources that you have as far as the staff and our head coach, and you pile your ideas together, and then you've got to narrow them down, and that's what we do. And we get a lot of good input from a lot of different ways, and that's fun. I mean, it's fun to work with the guys we work with and have the players that run those plays."

Pederson initially hired former Eagles wideout, Greg Lewis to be the receivers coach. Lewis was let go after their first season together, and Mike Groh was hired to take his place. Former first-round pick Nelson Agholor had a breakout season in 2017. A lot of it had to do with his hard work, but make no mistake, coach Groh was a part of the process as well. The passing game took off with Groh guiding the receivers. As a former quarterback, Groh was able to make the wideouts see the game through the eyes of the signal-caller.

"We are lucky to have coach Mike Groh because he is able to talk to us like a quarterback," Smith explained during Super Bowl media week. "As a former QB in college, we are able to learn things from the way he is talking. Even when we are not with the quarterbacks, we are being taught exactly how they are thinking and how to be in the right spot at the right time."

Nelson Agholor

Keith Allison

Groh shed some light on what it means to help a receiver see the game from a quarterback's perspective. "I try to teach guys the body language that quarterbacks are very comfortable with…what's attractive to them and how they can present themselves as the most open target that they can be. How do I present myself as the most open target, so I am more likely to get the ball," Groh said.

Pederson also decided to hold on to some of the tenured coaches that had been in Philadelphia under previous regimes. One of them was former teammate Duce Staley. Staley was a beloved player in Philadelphia because of his workman-like approach to the game. He was retained as running backs coach. One of the best things Staley was able to do was bring balance to the running backs room. Everyone knew their role and accepted the fact that they would not get 20 to 30 carries per game.

That was even the case for an established veteran such as LeGarrette Blount. "I can't say enough about Duce just for the simple fact of how well I was coached there and how he helped me understand things," Blount said shortly before he signed with the Detroit Lions. "I feel like Duce is one of the best RB coaches. He's one of the best coaches I've ever had in my entire life. I want to be a part of that for a while, so we will see how it goes."

The coaching staff that Pederson put together was well-equipped to go against the mighty Bill Belichick and the Patriots in Super Bowl LII.

7

A Father's Influence

Pederson's first football coach was his father, Gordon. Playing for his father presented a different set of challenges from the other kids on his team. "He always had high expectations for my brothers and me, and he coached us a little bit different than the rest of the team. I just think having that same mentality with the guys, just sort of a tough-love mentality with the guys now and having that relationship with them is something my dad and I had," Pederson said.

"He was positive and uplifting, but at the same time wanted to make sure we were doing things right and if we weren't, we would hear about it. That's kind of the same way how I treat what I'm doing today."

Getting the chance to follow in his father's footsteps is something that Pederson cherished. Unfortunately, the elder Pederson never got to see his son coach during the regular season. Pederson's father, Gordon, passed away on September 2, 2016. It was just over a week before Pederson was set to make his regular-season debut in the season opener against the Cleveland Browns. While his father was around, Pederson was able to lead the Eagles to a 4 – 0 record in the preseason. Doug's father may not have seen Pederson coach a regular season game, but he also never saw his son lose a game as an NFL head coach!

Not having his father there with him during the week leading up to the Super Bowl was tough for Pederson. "I think about him all the time, especially at this time of year. He would love to be a part of these games to be coming to this game, being it's a chance to play for the Super Bowl and all of that," Pederson said. "It's definitely been on my mind and the kinds of things, he might say to me."

8

Bradford and Wentz
—The Perfect Storm

Besides forming a coaching staff, one of the principal things Pederson had to get taken care of was selecting a quarterback. Sam Bradford had finished the 2015 season with 3,725 passing yards to go along with 19 touchdowns and 14 interceptions. He completed 65 percent of his passes as well. Bradford was about to hit the free agent market before being re-signing with the Eagles in March. The deal was worth $36 million over two years. With Bradford entrenched as the quarterback, the goal was to have him hold down the quarterback position while Pederson and the coaching staff developed his successor. The Eagles even had Cowboys quarterback Dak Prescott in their facility for a pre-draft visit. They came away from the visit thoroughly impressed with Prescott, but there was another player that stole their heart.

While at the Senior Bowl and the Combine, the team became enamored with Carson Wentz. As they spent more time with Wentz, they continued to grow fonder of him. The Eagles acquired the number eight overall pick in the 2016 draft from the Dolphins in exchange for linebacker Kiko Alonso and cornerback Byron Maxwell, plus the number thirteen overall pick. That move allowed them to clear out two unwanted players and their contracts.

Roseman traded the number eight pick along with a third- and a fourth-round selection in the 2016 NFL Draft, a first-round pick in 2017, and a second-round pick in 2018 to the Cleveland Browns for the number two pick in 2016 and a conditional fourth-round pick in 2017. Now armed with the second pick in the draft, the Eagles were in perfect position to get Wentz knowing the Rams were going to select Jared Goff with number one pick. Things seemed to be in order for everyone, except for Bradford.

Bradford felt betrayed and actually left the team's offseason workouts when he heard about the trade. Bradford reportedly asked for a trade as well. Once Wentz got into the building, he and Bradford found a way to coexist and actually get along. Their quarterback room was bolstered by the addition of Chase Daniel who was signed before Wentz was selected.

All three of them felt they should be the starter. They split reps evenly in mini-camp. Pederson went out of his way to praise Bradford as he started to emerge as a starter. "I look at what Sam's done, and he's taken this thing and run with it. It's unbelievable what he's done," Pederson said during an offseason press conference. "I'm so excited about the direction he's going, and the stuff that he's doing on the field right now are the things that I expected and what I saw at the end of the season last year from Sam Bradford."

Pederson and the Eagles headed to training camp with Bradford as the starter. Bradford connected with receivers using his pinpoint accuracy while Wentz showcased his big arm as he completed passes down the field to his wide receivers. The two were competing intensely despite their contrasting styles of play. Wentz made his debut in the preseason opener against the Tampa Bay Buccaneers. He was injured in the game and missed the rest of the preseason due to a hairline fracture in his ribs.

The team was preparing for the season opener against the Browns with Bradford as the starter. Just before the season began, Minnesota Vikings quarterback Teddy Bridgewater suffered a gruesome knee injury. The Vikings had what they felt was a championship-worthy roster in place. Losing Bridgewater put Minnesota in desperation mode. That was when Vikings GM Rich Speilman got on the phone with Eagles GM Howie Roseman. Speilman presented Roseman with an offer he couldn't refuse.

"We felt like this was an opportunity for us not only now but going forward that we had to take advantage of," Roseman said at a press conference on September 3. "Our plan wasn't to trade Sam Bradford. This trade offer from the Vikings changed things. This was not our blueprint or original plan. As we looked at the offer and what it could do for our team going forward, we felt like it was the best thing to do for our football team."

Speilman agreed to send the Vikings' first-round pick (number 14 overall) to the Eagles in exchange for Bradford. The deal was announced and just like that Carson Wentz was named the starter for the season opener. "It was pretty crazy. We just came off of the Indianapolis Colts preseason game, and Sam [Bradford] had a tremendous game," Pederson said. "Carson was ready to go. I picked up the phone and called him. I asked him how he felt about going into Week One as the starter, and he said, 'Let's go, Coach. Let's roll.'"

Wentz had only played in one preseason game as a rookie. He also missed valuable time during training camp with the sore ribs. The primary formula for his recovery was to rest. Throwing a football puts a lot of stress on the core which is where the ribs are located. It really came down to Wentz's pain threshold. Despite being thrust into starting duties, Wentz got off to a good start and led the Eagles to a win in Pederson's first game as a head coach.

9

Establishing the Right Culture and Building Trust

Pederson quickly made a name for himself because of his willingness to go for it on fourth down. It didn't always work in his first season, and Pederson fell under intense scrutiny from the media.

The fourth-down attempts that stick out the most came in a 28 – 23 road-loss to the Giants in Week Nine. Pederson elected to go for it on fourth and two from the Giants' 23-yard line.

Down 14 – 3 at the time, Pederson called a read-option play that was stopped causing a turnover on downs. Sending kicker Caleb Sturgis out to attempt a 40-yard field goal was a more high-percentage play and would have made the score 14 – 6.

Keith Allison

Zach Ertz

The Eagles were down 21 – 10 later in the game and faced a fourth and one on the Giants' six-yard line. Pederson wanted to go for the first down and then the touchdown instead of settling for a field goal. He elected to give the ball to Darren Sproles on an inside run, but they came up short. They left points on the board once again, but the message was clear. Pederson trusted his team and was willing to take risks with them.

"I'm going to continue to show confidence in our guys and believe in our guys," Pederson said after the game.

Given another chance to go for it on fourth down, Pederson once again showed trust in his players. This time it came later in the game with six minutes to go, and the Eagles were behind 28 – 20. Wentz hit Jordan Matthews for a 25-yard gain on fourth and nine to get the first down. They eventually had to settle for a field goal on the drive and lost the game by a score of 28 – 23. Although they lost the game, in the grand scheme of things, it would pay off in the end. That was the message Pederson delivered to the media during his post-game press conference.

"I think I'll stay aggressive. These are all part of our growth process on offense. Rookie quarterback, young receivers, veteran offensive line. So at the same time, we're trying to build this thing. We're trying to do it right," Pederson explained. "And by putting them in these situations, they're going to be better for this. They're going to be better down the stretch—somewhere it's going to pay off for us; it's going to pay off for all of us. So I'm going to continue being as aggressive as I can and send a message to our football team that I trust them.

"I feel like if I don't trust the guys—the team, the players—how are they going to believe in me as their coach? I put a lot of ownership on the team this past season and on myself in making sure that I would maintain that aggressiveness throughout the whole season."

The Eagles were faced with a similar situation later in the season when they were on the road against the Baltimore Ravens. Down by seven points with four seconds left in the game, Wentz scored on a four-yard run to pull within one point of tying the game. Pederson decided to go for a two-point conversion and the win instead of an extra-point attempt to tie the game and force it to overtime. The two-point conversion failed when Wentz's pass intended for Jordan Matthews was broken up by a Ravens defender. Philadelphia lost the game by a score of 27 – 26. It was their fifth consecutive loss.

After the game, the players showed their support for Pederson's aggressive play call. "I loved it. Our coach is aggressive, and he believed in us. We thought they were going to blitz, and they did. It was a good call, but they made a good play," Wentz said.

"Everyone on the team was behind the decision. We had them back on their heels, and we had the momentum," safety Malcolm Jenkins said after the game. "The last drive, we moved the ball very well, so I thought it was a good decision."

Putting the ball in his playmaker's hands with aggressive play calls earned the player's trust. They knew that if Pederson trusted them to come through on fourth down, he had confidence in them as players.

Tight end Zach Ertz touched on how Pederson's aggressive playcalling rubs off on the players when he was asked about it during Super Bowl media week. "Doug exudes confidence with all of us. Even last year when we weren't as successful on the fourth downs. He instilled that confidence in us to set the stage for this year," Ertz explained. "He wasn't going to leave anything in his pocket at the end of the game. He is going to trust us to make plays when opportunity calls. His ability to trust us instilled that confidence in us that no matter what the situation is, we will be successful. He is a phenomenal coach. As players, we love playing for him."

Former Eagles quarterback coach John DeFilippo was named the offensive coordinator for the Minnesota Vikings before the 2018 season. Having spent two seasons with Pederson, he got to see firsthand how the coach was willing to take risks with the aggressive playcalling. That is something that DeFilippo will surely take with him to the Vikings. It's a way to show the team that, as players, they have the trust of their coach.

"He's fearless. I have learned a lot from Doug. He stays on the attack. He is a creative play caller, but he is fearless. He is not afraid to put his foot on the gas," DeFilippo said during Super Bowl media availability. "He is by far the best playcaller that I've been around. When you see us go for two or go for it on fourth down at times, it shows. I think he has a lot of faith in the football team. He believes in our scheme. He is a fantastic playcaller."

The first season gave Pederson a body of work to learn from as a head coach. He figured the best way to approach things was to take advantage of every opportunity to the fullest. "My mentality, my philosophy is this opportunity is only going to come around probably once. I am going to make the most of it. I am going to do what is right for our football team and make sure our guys are in the best position to be successful," Pederson explained. "After my first season, I went back and studied the play calls. I studied how I called the games, how I approached games as far as studying and getting myself ready to play. I think that's a big advantage to be able to do that after the first year of calling plays for the entire season."

A Collaborative Effort

No one on the coaching staff sought credit for the team's success. It was always a group effort. Pederson, DeFilippo, and Frank Reich came together with wide receivers coach Mike Groh to put together the passing game plan while running backs Duce Staley and offensive line coach Jeff Stoutland chipped in on the running game.

"The background that all of the coaches have helps us tremendously. There is a ton of knowledge on our offensive staff. That's a tribute to Doug Pederson for the staff that he hired," DeFilippo said after they won the Super Bowl. "It's unique. Coach did a great job of hiring guys that have a personality where no one needs the credit. Our credit was being at the Super Bowl. He put great minds together, guys that have low egos and that are team players. We ask our players to buy into a team atmosphere so why not our coaches too.

"It starts with Doug and how he's such an approachable guy and opens to new ideas. It rubs off on the players. They see how much our coaching staff enjoys being around each other and teaching the game."

The game plan was a collaboration. Coaches were encouraged to go out and find plays to add to each week's list of plays to be called. Pederson had his core group of plays that were staples of the offense, but different concepts could be implemented each week according to the team they were facing.

Giving the coaching staff an opportunity to have a great deal of input not only challenged them, it inspired them as well. "What I take from my time there was, I really like the collaborative effort," Reich said at the NFL Scouting Combine. "I think, the more coaches we get involved, . . . somebody's got to make a decision, and that's what the head coach does. That's what the coordinator does. You make decisions, but, you get ideas, and you talk things through. I think that makes you better.

"You've got to do it in creative ways because you have limited time to prepare. But, that's why you work so hard to hire the best staff so you can get the bestsellers ideas from the best people to help you win."

It takes a great deal of confidence to be willing to step aside and allow a coach to make suggestions or add his flavor to the game plan. The way Pederson gave his coaches the liberty to add their flare created more trust with them, in the end forming an offense that couldn't be stopped. When the Eagles faced the Patriots in Super Bowl LII, they presented a balanced attack. Patriots head coach Bill Belichick was known for taking what a team did best away.

The problem with the Eagles offense is they were a collaborative effort just like the coaching staff was. Any given week could see a different player lead the team in receiving or rushing yards. Reich likened them to a basketball team that has a bunch of players that can go out and score 20 points. The offense was so balanced that Belichick couldn't put together a scheme to take a specific part of it away without risking being defeated by something else.

If there was any team primed to hand the Patriots another loss in a Super Bowl, it was the Eagles. They didn't have a 1,000-yard rusher to take away, and there wasn't a 1,000-yard receiver. Instead, they ran through opponent after opponent as a team. It was indeed a collaborative effort.

Emotional Intelligence

Offensive coordinator Frank Reich summed up Pederson's approach to coaching the players perfectly: "Doug had a great way about him in his ability to be a player's coach, but they also knew that he was in charge. I think that's the balance that you're always looking to strike," Reich said.

Emotional intelligence is defined as "the capacity to be aware of, control, and express one's emotions, and to handle interpersonal relationships judiciously and empathetically." This is something that team owner Jeffrey Lurie looked for in his next head coach after the impersonal days of Chip Kelly. Lurie wanted the players to feel like they were a part of something. Lurie and the Eagles hit the jackpot when they hired Pederson. Pederson knew he had to get the players to buy into the culture that he wanted to establish.

He leaned on his days as a player as he installed his plan to get the players to support his philosophy.

"Fourteen years in the locker room. I understand the players—the dynamic of what's in that locker room. To know what goes on down there and how these guys interact, you come across a lot of things. I am able to relate to them," Pederson explained the week before Super Bowl LII.

Like any relationship, having an open line of communication is vital. It has to be a two-way street. That's precisely what Pederson established in Philadelphia. "You hear all the time 'He's a player's coach' whatever that might be. I think you have to listen to your guys. In today's game, communication is big with me," Pederson said. "I have to make guys understand where I am coming from, and I have to understand where they are coming from. That's why I did a player's committee of veteran players that we can communicate with back and forth. That's probably the biggest reason for that buy-in. It comes down to being honest and open with guys."

The veteran's committee was a sounding board for the players regarding everything from putting the pads on during practice to dealing with personal issues in the locker room. Wisely, Pederson allowed the players to 'self-police' the locker room but with understanding and respect for the culture that he wanted in place.

Setting the Tone

The Eagles came out firing on all cylinders in Pederson's regular-season debut against the woeful Cleveland Browns. They achieved perfect balance on offense. Led by running back Ryan Mathews's 77 rushing yards, Philadelphia gained a total of 133 yards on the ground. Paired with Carson Wentz's 278-yard passing day, the Eagles seemed to be off to a great start.

Even though it was his first game as an NFL head coach, Pederson's focus was more on getting Wentz, and the team itself settled into a rhythm to start things off. "I wanted to get him [Wentz], and really the offensive line, settled into the football game. First two plays, we wanted to run the ball with potential throws attached to it, and then really just sort of let the game unfold from there. The other thing, too, was get Carson kind of on the perimeter, where he does some of his best work outside the pocket," Pederson said after the game. "And then, you know, we got down into the red zone, and he made a great throw to Jordan in the back of the end zone for the touchdown to finish it off. Again, wanted to get him in there comfortable. Get our offensive line just sort of rolling off the ball and eventually build up to some more down-the-field stuff."

The next game came on the road. Pederson worked to establish tempo for the offense in their road debut which came in Week Two in Chicago against the Bears. Pederson dialed up six consecutive passes by Wentz to open the game. After converting on a fourth and two, Pederson called for a running play by Darren Sproles.

The offense opened the game with a sense of urgency that seemed to take the Bears by surprise. However, a sack by Bears defensive end Sam Acho forced the Eagles to kick a field goal. Philadelphia ended up beating the Bears by a score of 29 – 14. Pederson then led the Eagles to a convincing home 34 – 3 home win over the Pittsburgh Steelers. The win gave Philadelphia a 3 – 0 record heading into the bye week.

Pederson suffered his first regular-season loss in Week Five when they fell to the Detroit Lions by a score of 24 – 23. During the bye week,

Eagles linebacker Nigel Bradham was arrested for bringing a loaded gun to the airport.

Pederson was faced with his first decision regarding disciplining a player for misconduct. Bradham had been arrested and charged with assaulting a hotel employee in Miami before the 2016 season also. While the reason was never officially made public, Bradham was held out of the first half of the Lions game. Detroit jumped out to a 21 – 7 lead at one point in the first half when Bradham was out. The Lions only scored three points in the second half, coincidentally, after Bradham was inserted back into the lineup.

Bradham's situation wasn't the only off-the-field incident for the Eagles in Pederson's first season as head coach. Just a month later, then-wide receiver Josh Huff was arrested and charged with possessing an unloaded nine millimeter handgun without a permit, a magazine that had six hollow-point bullets, and a small amount of marijuana in November of 2016.

"[I'm] obviously disappointed. It's not what you want on a player day off to see happen," Pederson said in a press conference after learning about Huff's arrest. "He and I spoke about it privately, and it's one of the things I talk about all the time with players. You just try to eliminate distractions and take care of your business outside of the building. He understands. Obviously, it's out of our hands at this point. We just got to see where it goes." Philadelphia released Huff the next day. The Eagles proceeded to lose six of the next seven games.

Bolstered by right tackle Lane Johnson's return from a 10-game suspension, Philadelphia won their final two games to end the season. Johnson's return made Philadelphia much better up front. They ran the ball effectively once again. There was hope for them entering 2017.

"I'll tell you just how well these guys fought the entire season, all the way down to the end," Pederson said after the season finale. "I challenged the team a couple weeks ago as far as let's finish the season the right way, and our last month of the season has been definitely heading in the right direction. It's great to finish strong, two division opponents, and get two wins this way. Kicking off the year the right way."

Little did Pederson know, the Eagles were about to make Philadelphia history the following season.

Picking up Where He Left Off

After finishing the 2016 season with a 3 – 0 record, Pederson had big expectations for the Eagles. Adding wide receiver coach Mike Groh, along with free agent wide receivers Alshon Jeffery and Torrey Smith, was expected to help the passing game become more lethal. The new additions had a significant impact on wide receiver Nelson Agholor. Coupled with Agholor's new day by day approach, and the free agent additions, Philadelphia's passing game was set to explode in 2017.

Pederson focused on situational football during the offseason. The coaching staff worked on becoming more efficient on third downs and in the red zone. They dedicated stretches of practice to specific situations to focus on getting better in each given area. Quarterback coach John DeFilippo worked with Wentz on extending plays and looking for receivers to get open down the field. Groh and the receivers, along with the tight ends, worked on uncovering themselves when the play broke down.

The results showed in the first game of the regular season, a 30 – 17 win over the Washington Redskins. Wentz's first touchdown pass came on a play in which he was able to break the pocket before spotting Agholor turning his route up the field. Wentz heaved a deep pass to Agholor who caught the ball and eluded Redskins safety D.J. Swearinger for a 58-yard touchdown. The Eagles put the NFC East on notice with their convincing win over Washington which broke a five-game losing streak to their division rival that dated back to 2014.

The following week was a case of student vs. teacher as Pederson's Eagles went to Kansas City to face Andy Reid and the Chiefs. Reid was sure Pederson would have the Eagles ready to give them a challenge in Week Two. "I have a lot of respect for him, and I think he's doing a nice job there. I know he'll have his team ready, and they'll come in here," Reid said during the week leading up to the game against the Eagles. "He's got a good football team, he's got good coaches, so they'll come in and be ready to go. Once you start the game, though, you're playing the game, and it really doesn't necessarily matter who's over there."

Pederson was facing Reid for the first time as a coach. It was evident to Pederson that going against Reid in itself would create an additional set of problems if he allowed it to. "Listen, Andy Reid teams are well-prepared, as we know, and we've got to do the same thing this week. We've just got to be ultra-prepared," Pederson during a press conference leading up to the Chiefs game. "It just comes down to the preparation and hard work for them. And that's what [Reid] has done in the past. And I think sometimes, in my position, I don't want to put any added pressure on myself to perform. . . . For me, I can't get caught up in that record. I can't get caught up in who's on the other sideline. But it will be fun to get out there. Once we tee it up and kick it off, it's all about the business and all about the game."

Pederson had to fight the temptation to place too much importance on beating his sensei. Every time he looked across the field, Reid was standing there looking back. Having spent time in Kansas City, Pederson was well aware of the home field advantage that Arrowhead Stadium presents for the Chiefs. "That is a tough place to play, now. It is a loud, loud place and we've got to be able to handle that crowd noise. We've got to do it through

Carson Wentz

communication, nonverbal communication. All that has to be on-point this week in practice," Pederson explained.

The Eagles came close but fell short against the Chiefs by a touchdown. It was a tough game for the team, but they proved they could compete with anyone by hanging with one of the best teams on the road.

The next week against the Giants was a sign that it may be the Eagles' year. They were in a dogfight against their divisional rival from the north. The game appeared to be headed for overtime with the score tied 24 – 24 and 13 seconds remaining on the clock. Philadelphia took over on their own 38-yard line after forcing New York to punt.

Instead of letting the time run out and go into overtime at home, Pederson elected to attack the Giants and go for the win. Wentz's first pass fell incomplete. With seven seconds left in the game, Wentz found Alshon Jeffery on a 17-yard outbreaking route. Jeffery secured the catch and stepped out of bounds at the Giants' 43-yard line, leaving just one second on the clock. Pederson sent out rookie kicker Jake Elliott to attempt a 61-yard field goal to win the game. Elliott promptly drilled the kick to win the game for the Eagles and set a franchise record for the longest field goal made.

"Quite honestly, I had so much confidence standing there—calmness. I had just watched him kick a couple kickoffs extremely deep into the end zone," Pederson said after the game. "It was pretty awesome. Sounded like a cannon off his foot. Great snap, great hold, the protection was there.

"With time and only one timeout, we were trying to get as close as we could, but we felt that if we were outside of that, about where we were, we were going to at least attempt it."

The heart-stopping win over the Giants kick-started a nine-game win streak that saw the Eagles dominate their opponents along the way. They outscored opposing teams by a whopping 154 points. A trip to Seattle to face the Seahawks was the biggest test for the Eagles since their matchup against the Chiefs in Kansas City.

"I think this is a great opportunity for our football team. I've heard things this week and the last couple of weeks that things have been kind of sort of easy for us," Pederson said two days before facing the Seahawks. "This is the National Football League, and nothing is easy. These games coming up will definitely be a benchmark for our football team.

"And it's a great challenge, on the road, playoff environment against a great football team that knows how to win, and they know how to win in the fourth quarter. We've just got to go up there and do our jobs, be prepared, handle the noise, but [it's] a great opportunity for our team at this time of the year."

For just the second time in 13 weeks, the Eagles fell short. This time the score was 24 — 10. Both losses came on the road in extremely tough environments. The next tough situation the team would have to face was one that could have broken Pederson and the Eagles.

12

<u>Winning without Carson</u>

The Eagles season could have been derailed when Carson Wentz went down with torn ligaments in his knee during a Week Fourteen game against the Los Angeles Rams in 2017. Wentz injured the knee as he tried to dive into the end zone to score a touchdown late in the third quarter.

The Eagles were down 28 – 24 and Wentz remained in the game after tearing the ligaments. He hung in there for one more play in which he connected with Alshon Jeffery on a two-yard touchdown pass. The score put the Eagles ahead 31 – 28. Wentz walked off the field and directly to the trainer's tent. After a brief examination, Wentz was taken into the locker room.

The Rams were able to take the lead back on a one-yard touchdown plunge by running back Todd Gurley II. Gurley's touchdown made the score 35 – 31. Having taken over for Wentz, backup quarterback Nick Foles led the Eagles on a 10-play, 52-yard drive that resulted in a 41-yard field goal by Jake Elliott that made the score 35 – 34. A sack/fumble by Eagles defensive end Chris Long set up another field goal by Elliott that put Philadelphia ahead 37 – 35. The defense forced the Rams to punt, giving the Eagles the ball back with just over two minutes left in the game to protect their lead. Desperately in need of a first down, Foles connected with Nelson Agholor on a nine-yard pass on third and eight.

The Rams were forced to use their second timeout and only had one remaining while the Eagles had a fresh set of downs. Philadelphia ended up winning the game 43 – 35, scoring another touchdown on a 16-yard fumble return by defensive end Brandon Graham. The win meant the Eagles were NFC East champions and going to the postseason for the first time since 2013 when Foles was previously the starting quarterback.

Pederson confirmed that Wentz had suffered a torn ACL after the game. He vowed to rally the troops around Foles and the rest of the team. His reaction to questions about whether or not the team would be able to recover from the loss of Wentz was telling. "Heck yeah! We can overcome this. We overcame a pro-bowl left tackle. We overcame our middle linebacker. We've overcome our running back. We've overcome a core special teams player this year. [We've overcome] our kicker this year," Pederson said during his post-game press conference. "This is no different. Yeah, he is the quarterback of our football team. Each one of these guys that I mentioned is tough to replace."

Giving Foles a public endorsement was just another one of the ways that Pederson was able to use his emotional intelligence to let his now starting quarterback know that he was willing to ride with him. "The reason we went out and got [QB] Nick Foles was for reasons like this and situations like this. I'm excited for Nick. I hate it for Carson Wentz. I hate it for the career, the season, I guess, that he's been having. But at the same time, it's been the next-man-up mentality, and that's how we approach it this week."

Pederson said he had some doubts when Wentz went down. It's only natural for a head coach to be shaken up after he lost a quarterback who was playing at an MVP level before being injured. But for Pederson, it was about the bigger picture. He knew there were other strengths on the team.

"I knew we had a tremendous defense, we can use our running game, and Nick is a veteran quarterback. A lot of things were going for us at the time. We had just won the NFC East, we punched our ticket to the postseason. We were still in good shape. That was the reality," Pederson said before leaving for the Super Bowl in Minnesota. "Maybe in here there was a little doubt, but I would never do that in front of the team or in the media. For me at that time, it didn't take long for me to fire back up."

Foles's first start of the season came against the Giants. Pederson felt right about Foles as they prepared for their Week Fifteen matchup. "I think he's definitely matured as a quarterback [in terms of] his leadership ability and his understanding of our offense and of defenses. We always knew he was a very smart, intellectual quarterback and could process information," Pederson said during a press conference before the game. "He's been able to take it to the next level in his preparation and just how he responds to the guys and how the guys have responded to him."

The way Foles responded when he came in to relieve Wentz the previous week stood out to Pederson. He pointed to how the players had confidence in Foles despite not getting extensive game time with him during the earlier games. Foles opened the Giants game with an easy throw to wide receiver Alshon Jeffery which went for 12-yards. That drive went 75 yards in seven plays and was capped off by a three-yard touchdown pass from Foles to Jeffery. As the game went on, Foles settled into a groove against the Giants. He completed 24 of his 38 pass attempts for 237 yards and four touchdowns.

Things got a little shaky in the next game. The Eagles offense sputtered for most of the game and Foles struggled to make plays. Foles threw his first interception of the year against the Raiders. However, when it mattered the most, Foles found a way to advance the ball into field goal range. Foles connected with Nelson Agholor on consecutive plays for a total of 13 yards. Tight end Zach Ertz was next with successive receptions leading to Philadelphia having the ball at the Raiders' 31-yard line. Jake Elliott booted a 48-yard field goal, and the Eagles took a 13 – 10 lead. Just like the previous week against the Rams, Foles came through in the clutch, and the defense ended the game with a fumble return for a touchdown. This time it was rookie Derek Barnett with the scoop and score that covered 23 yards.

With the win, the Eagles clinched a home field advantage in the playoffs. The road to the Super Bowl in Minnesota had to go through Lincoln Financial Field.

Foles started the final regular season game but only played a couple of series before giving way to backup Nate Sudfeld. He opened the game on fire having completed three straight passes before his fourth throw fell incomplete. A third down pass intended for Torrey Smith was dropped, which killed the drive. Foles came out a few series later, but there were some doubts from the fans and media based on his performance against the Raiders and briefly against the Cowboys.

After the game, Pederson fielded questions about Foles but true to form, he backed his quarterback. "I'm not concerned. I've still got a lot of confidence in our offense. Again, it's not one person or one guy. There is enough to go around," Pederson said. "It's tough in this situation where you know you're kind of maybe only going to get a quarter, maybe a couple series, and you're coming out. But I've still got a lot of confidence in the guys."

He pointed to the opening drive as an example of how Foles moved the ball. "We had a huge drop on a third down that would've kept the drive alive," Pederson said.

No matter what, Pederson had to make sure Foles was as confident as can be heading to the playoffs. The offensive scheme that Pederson uses incorporates a lot of read-pass-option plays (RPOs). Foles has to be in the right frame of mind to make a quick decision whether or not to throw the ball or hand it off. Having any kind of hesitation will foil either decision, even if it's the right one. Pederson reiterated how crucial it was for Foles to make the right decisions after their playoff win over the Falcons in the divisional round. It was a hard-fought game that ended with a goal-line stand by the Eagles to protect a 15 – 10 lead.

He praised Foles for how he was able to find Jeffery on the sideline for a 15-yard gain to set up a 53-yard field goal by Jake Elliott. It pulled Philadelphia to within one point just before halftime. "Just him making great decisions and getting the ball out of his hand and finding the open receiver. He did a really nice job executing the game plan how we, and how I, know Nick can," Pederson said after the game.

Being a number one seed in the playoffs and still having the underdog status placed on the team bothered Pederson, even though he didn't want to admit it. The way so many analysts wanted to write the Eagles off after Carson Wentz was hurt didn't go unnoticed by Pederson. He finally pushed back at those who counted them out when he spoke after the divisional playoff win.

"Since that point [Wentz's injury], no one has given us a chance. And I understand, Carson's a great player, but every week, our guys are hearing the same thing; that now we are all of a sudden not good enough," Pederson said emphatically. "We're 13 – 3 and have the best record in football, we've got home-field advantage throughout. Listen, there's not a lot—I mean, the guys are going to motivate themselves just based on what they have done and heard for the last month of football.

"Listen, it really doesn't matter what you guys talk about because that locker room in there is united and I'll go to bat for every one of those guys, and I'll go to war with every one of those guys in that dressing room."

The underdog role continued the following week in the NFC Championship game, even though it was taking place in Philadelphia at Lincoln Financial Field. The Minnesota Vikings were coming to town with a defense that was expected to shut down Pederson's offense.

Pederson sent a message to Foles through the media. It basically told him to keep things simple and execute the offense. "The message is still the same: Go be Nick," Pederson said the Friday before the NFC Championship game. "Feed off of last week, obviously, but it's a different set of challenges, a different team. You don't have to force anything. Let the offense work for you."

During the week leading up to the NFC Championship game, Pederson said he sensed a great deal of confidence from Foles during practice. Facing the Vikings' top-rated defense was no easy task, but Foles was up for the challenge. Pederson gave Foles the opportunity to turn it loose against Minnesota. He dialed up 33 passing plays for Foles. The result was 26 completions for 352 yards and three touchdowns. Foles was lights-out against the Vikings. He connected with Alshon Jeffery for a 53-yard touchdown in which he was able to maneuver within the pocket before stepping up and launching a beautiful pass as Jeffery turned up the field.

Perhaps the most significant play came on a flea-flicker that Pederson timed perfectly with the play call. After a couple of short passes along with runs by Jay Ajayi and LeGarrette Blount, Pederson called for the trick play. Foles handed the ball off to Corey Clement who pitched it back to Foles. Torrey Smith streaked down the left sideline after a slow release from the line of scrimmage and Foles unleashed a perfectly placed ball that landed right in Smith's hands as he dove across the goal line. The score blew the game open.

"Those plays, you just don't—like grasping at straws out of thin air— you don't just pull them out and think, 'I'm going to run it this week.' There's got to be a reason for running a gadget play," Pederson said. "I just felt that as I game-planned this week and studied our formations and some of the things that we did, [I] felt like we'd get an opportunity to at least attempt the play. Great execution, protection was there. Nick did a great job of stepping up and sliding right. And then what a finish. What a catch by [WR] Torrey [Smith], and right in the front corner of the end zone. And it is great when they work."

Foles delivered in a big way. Pederson had plenty of praise for Foles after the game. "My hat's off to Nick. Trusting in his ability, trusting in me as the head coach and putting him in ideal situations and situations to be successful on the field," Pederson said during a post-game press conference. "Then for the guys. The guys to believe in him. Listen, he's not a rookie. He's a veteran player who has played a lot of games in this league.

"He's started a lot of games. He had a Pro Bowl year a couple years ago. So this is not a rookie we're talking about. Just so happy for him and what he's been through and everything now to finally . . . help this football team get to where we want to go and hopefully finish the year right."

The celebration in Philadelphia was grand, but the team knew they had an even more significant job to do in Minnesota.

13

<u>Super Bowl LII</u>

Super Bowl LII

Arash Arabasadi

Before the NFC Championship game, the Eagles knew they would be facing the almighty New England Patriots if they beat the Minnesota Vikings. It was going to be a rematch of Super Bowl XXXIX in 2004 when New England handed the Eagles their second Super Bowl loss in franchise history.

Pederson wanted his guys to make sure they didn't get too caught up in the moment. He wanted them to enjoy their time in Minnesota but make sure they brought the intensity in practice. "We've got a game to play, and it's not a vacation next week. My message to the team is just that," Pederson said before leaving for Minnesota. "We're going to prepare this week as if we're playing this weekend, obviously, and then we can sort of fine-tune some things. But we've just got to stay on top of our game, keep the grind, and keep the intensity going right into next week."

The two teams had a different demeanor during Super Bowl week. Philadelphia made sure they soaked up the moment, while the Patriots had a more business-like mindset.

The contrasting approaches to the week were evident from the start at media night. Patriots head coach Bill Belichick wore a suit, complete with a shirt and tie to media night. On the other hand, Pederson showed up wearing jeans and an Eagles polo.

"Our guys just go about their business every day. We know what we are going against," Pederson said during his Super Bowl opening press conference. "We have a lot of respect for the Patriots, but it is about what we do, how we go about this week. Eliminate the noise and the distractions. Guys get pulled in a lot of different directions. There are a lot of obligations but as we begin the work week. We just try to be flexible, and whatever we are asked to do, we do, but we want to make sure we stay on task."

The players followed suit. Right tackle Lane Johnson was at the podium with a pair of John Lennon-like sunglasses on along with a striped beanie hat. Defensive end Brandon Graham did an interview with a dog mask on. To some, it may have seemed like they were having too much fun, but for them, it was just a way to not let the moment get too big. It was a way to stay relaxed.

Some players did not seem to enjoy the week as much as others. Take wide receiver Alshon Jeffery for instance. If he had it his way, there wouldn't be so much build up for the Super Bowl. "My advice, man, we could cut out all this and just play football. I'm a guy who wishes we could've stayed in Philly and stick to our routine and just come out here on Friday," Jeffery said the Thursday before the Super Bowl.

The mystique of the Patriots is something that Pederson refused to get caught up in.

"My mind is on the Patriots and focused on the scheme and trying to figure out how to beat them. That's the bottom line. How to get my team prepared to play the final game of the season, and that's where my mind is right now," Pederson said during a Super Bowl press conference.

"It's important for us to make sure that we continue to detail what we do in practice, [and] we execute our game plan. Guys are focused that way. And you just can't get caught up in what they do. It's more about what we do in this game."

At the end of the day, Pederson's goal was simply to stay aggressive and call his game. "You have to study every situation and understand how they will attack you and how you should attack them," Pederson explained. "You can't give them opportunities, limit turnovers against a quarterback like Tom Brady. You have to play for sixty minutes. You have to play a full ballgame against those guys. There's no panic. They just stay the course. They execute their game plan."

Perhaps the wittiest of all Pederson's pre-Super Bowl strategies was what many perceived to be a fake walkthrough practice in US Bank Stadium before the Super Bowl. Opposing teams had become skeptical of the Patriots after 'Spygate' in 2007 when they were caught taping the Jets' sideline signals during a game. "I think there are still a lot of coaches out there that don't trust the Patriots, so sometimes they'll overthink it and do some fake plays in case anybody's watching," Eagles safety Malcolm Jenkins said in an appearance on SportsCenter.

The practice was never confirmed to be a fake walkthrough, but judging from long snapper Rich Lovato's comments to 620 WDAE in Tampa back in February, it seems like it was just that. "We weren't going to show anything to anyone, especially being at the stadium," Lovato said soon after the Super Bowl. "I believe our whole walkthrough was just a complete fake walkthrough. We did it at the stadium. There were certain people walking around. . . . I believe I overheard someone say a lot of the plays we were running weren't even in the playbook for the Super Bowl."

One of the most critical plays for the Eagles was left out of the walkthrough to make sure it was a surprise when Pederson called for the offense to use it. That play is known as the 'Philly Special' and has become a historic play in Super Bowl history.

14

Philly Special

The play has become etched in Philadelphia sports history. Doug Pederson dialed up a trick play on fourth down in the biggest game of the Eagles career.

Affectionately known as the 'Philly Special,' this play involved a double reverse handoff followed by a pass to the quarterback. It is the kind of play that kids run when they are playing pickup football on the playground. Having the guts to make such a play call in the Super Bowl was typical of Pederson. He has been a risk taker since taking over as head coach of the Eagles.

Up by a score of 15 – 12, the Eagles were looking to answer a long touchdown drive by the Patriots. They drove all the way to the Patriots' one-yard line thanks in large part to a 55-yard catch and run by running back Corey Clement. Facing a fourth and one, Pederson elected to go for it instead of kicking the field goal.

"I kept remembering that you're playing Tom Brady and the New England Patriots," Pederson said after the game. "You have to score touchdowns. I said after the first couple of series of the game to the offensive staff that we can't keep kicking field goals."

There was no way Pederson was going to kick a field goal in that situation. It would have been a win for the Patriots, and they would have momentum going into halftime. Some of the special teams players were gearing up to go in on field goal team, but that was shot down quickly. "I was standing right there assuming that I had to go out for a field goal. I am right next to Doug, and he's pushing me back saying, 'No we are going for it,'" Eagles center Rich Lovato said in February on 620 WDAE radio in Tampa back. "Watching that pay unfold and run so perfectly during the Super Bowl, I was just in awe."

The Eagles called a timeout and Foles jogged over to the sideline to talk to Pederson. As Foles went to the sideline, he suggested they run the Philly Special.

"Do you want Philly, Philly?" Foles asked.

After the Super Bowl, Foles gave a little background on the play and why he felt it was the time to unleash it. "That's something we've been working on, and Doug [Pederson] and I were talking," Foles said during a post-game press conference. "I was like, 'Let's just run it.' It was a good time, and the end was a little wider than I thought, so I was like, 'I really need to sell like I'm not doing anything.'"

The timing was perfect for Foles to suggest the play. After a short pause, Pederson said, "Yeah, let's do it."

Pederson said he didn't plan on calling the Philly Special. They had a different play in place before the timeout was called. If it wasn't for the timeout, the Philly Special might not have been in existence as we know it today. "It was not a part of my thought process at all. The time on the clock was running out. We got out of the huddle late. Nick ran over, and we were looking at a couple of plays, a couple of plus-five red zone plays, some two-point plays in that situation," Pederson explained on the Rich Eisen show. "He whispered 'Philly Special,' and I just looked at him and we locked eyes, and I said, 'Let's go.' It was the perfect call at the right time of the game, and our guys executed it extremely well."

Pederson said the Philly special was a play they had in for about three weeks. They repped it against the Vikings and considered running it in the NFC Championship.

Like a real team player, Pederson refused to take credit for the play design and timing of making the play call. "Fearless or not, I trust my staff. There is a lot of collaboration that goes in to in. There's a lot of conversation. It's not just me calling plays," Pederson said. "There's a lot of dialogue behind the scenes that gives me the confidence to make the play calls. It's a team effort. I approach each game the same and try to stay as aggressive as possible but be smart."

Former Eagles offensive coordinator Frank Reich told Peter King of MMQB the play that became the Philly Special was found by then-assistant quarterback coach Press Taylor. One of Taylor's responsibilities is to stockpile trick plays from watching other teams in the league. Taylor found the play in a Week Sixteen matchup between the Vikings and Bears. Former Eagles quarterback Matt Barkley was on the receiving end of a pass thrown by wideout Cam Meredith.

Executing the play to perfection was the result of being dialed in. The Eagles had gone through the play during a walkthrough at their hotel, the Radisson Blu, but in total, they practiced the play maybe six times or so.

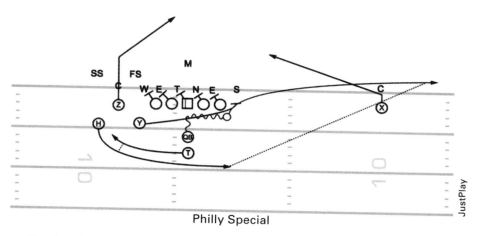

Philly Special

On the play, quarterback Foles moved behind his offensive line and the ball was directly snapped to running back Clement. Clement went on to pitch the ball to Burton, who passed the ball to a wide-open Foles for the touchdown.

The ball exchanged hands multiple times. Anytime multiple players handle the ball on a play, there is a high risk for a fumble. That wasn't the case for the Eagles. Foles became the first player in Super Bowl history to throw for a touchdown pass and catch a touchdown pass as well. Many analysts call this play one of the gutsiest play calls in Super Bowl history.

Scoring a touchdown instead of kicking a field goal was a four-point gain for Philadelphia. Going against a Brady-led offense that produced 613 yards of total offense, the Eagles were going to need every point they could get. Calling the Philly Special on fourth down was an example of Pederson's willingness to scratch and claw for every point they could get. That aggressiveness is what resulted in their Super Bowl victory.

Player Spotlight: The Offensive Line

There is no group that personified the Philadelphia Eagles more than their offensive line. Center Jason Kelce and right tackle Lane Johnson embraced the underdog mantra to the fullest. Kelce's epic speech at the end of the Super Bowl parade was one of the most memorable ever.

Jason Peters was told he was too old, didn't have it anymore. Before he got hurt, he was the best freakin tackle in the whole NFL. Steven Wisniewksi was told he didn't have it. Jason Kelce's too small. Lane Johnson can't lay off the juice. Brandon Brooks has anxiety. Carson Wentz didn't go to a Division I school. Nick Foles don't got it. Corey Clement's too slow. LeGarrette Blount aint got it anymore. Jay Ajayi can't stay healthy. Torrey Smith can't catch. Nelson Agholor can't catch. Zack Ertz can't block. Brent Celek's too old. Brandon Graham was drafted too high. Vinny Curry aint got it. Beau Allen can't fit the scheme. Mychal Kendricks can't fit the scheme. Nigel Bradham can't catch. Jalen Mills can't cover. Patrick Robinson can't cover. It's the whole team! It's the whole team!

This entire organization was a bunch of men driven to accomplish something. You're a bunch of underdogs! And you know what an underdog is? It's a hungry dog. And Jeff Stoutland has had this in our building for five years. It's a quote in the O-line room that has stood on the wall for the past five years: Hungry dogs run faster!

And that's this team. Bottom line is, we wanted it more. All the players, all the coaches, the front office, Jeffrey Lurie. Everybody wanted it more.

Kelce could not have said it any better. One of the many things that stood out about his speech was how he included each of his offensive linemates. The offensive line is one of the units on the Eagles that truly personifies the family atmosphere that exists in Philadelphia's locker room. When Jason Peters went down during their Super Bowl season, they rallied together to get Halapoulivaati Vaitai ready to step in at left tackle. Peters stayed with the team as he rehabbed his injury. He even walked to the middle of the field for the coin toss with the captains before games.

A struggling Isaac Seumalo gave way to Stefen Wisniewski at left guard, and the offense took off. Seumalo didn't sulk. Instead, he had an impact when Doug Pederson wanted to use a jumbo personnel package and add a sixth offensive lineman to the game.

Wisniewski didn't get a real opportunity to fight for a starting spot during training camp. Starting left tackle Allen Barbre was traded, and the job was given to Seumalo. Wisniewski kept pressing forward and took advantage when he was given the opportunity to play against the Kansas City Chiefs and New York Giants before being named the starter for the season.

They Were All Underdogs in Different Ways.

Kelce's underdog roots stem back to when he was a high school athlete looking to play at the next level. As a young kid growing up in Cleveland Heights, Ohio, Kelce played running back and linebacker. Kelce wasn't heavily recruited out of high school but managed to walk-on at Cincinnati as a running back. Kelce switched to fullback before making the final move which landed him on the offensive line. As a sophomore, Kelce started 13 games for a high-powered Bearcats offense that averaged 27.3 points and 375.3 yards of total offense per game.

Offensive Line

He was joined by his brother Travis at Cincinnati in 2008. Kelce was named to the All-Big East second team as a junior, helping lead his team to their second consecutive Big East Championship. After being a two-year starter at left guard, Kelce was moved to center his senior year. He responded by being named Honorable Mention All-American and second team All-Big East.

The underdog story continued when Kelce wanted to go to the NFL. At 6-foot-2, 280 pounds, Kelce wasn't the 'true NFL-size' center. The Eagles selected Kelce is the sixth round (number 191 overall) of the 2011 NFL Draft. Philadelphia knew precisely what they wanted to do with the undersized center thanks to their new offensive line coach Howard Mudd.

Mudd's last stop as an offensive line coach was with the Indianapolis Colts. That was where he got to work with center Jeff Saturday, another undersized center. The Colts liked to run stretch plays and take advantage of Saturday's athleticism by pulling him to the outside so he could escort running backs to the alley. When Mudd saw Kelce, he envisioned the same kind of success using outside zone concepts. Although Kelce was a late-round pick, he was in an intense competition with veteran Jamaal Jackson for a starting spot.

He earned the nickname 'Hedgehog' from fellow rookie offensive lineman Danny Watkins. Watkins called Kelce a hedgehog because of his spiky hair and bushy beard along with his quickness on the field. As training camp went on, Kelce started to pull ahead of Jackson on the depth chart. He started the third preseason game and was named the starting center for the regular season in late August. Kelce started all 16 games as a rookie, becoming the only center in team history to do so.

Kelce became known for his ability to get out in space and make blocks on the run. There wasn't a center in the league that could get to the second level of the defense and clear out a path as well as Kelce. His athleticism also showed in the screen game. Kelce was able to break down and take out defensive backs or agile linebackers that generally make offensive linemen miss.

In his second season, Kelce suffered a partially torn MCL and torn ACL in just the second week of the season. Kelce was placed on injured reserve and out for the year.

Philadelphia struggled to a 4 – 12 record with two of those wins coming when Kelce was in the lineup in the first two games. Offensive line coach Howard Mudd retired in 2012. Reid was fired after his worst season as a head coach. Chip Kelly was brought in to replace Reid. Kelly brought his up-tempo offense to Philadelphia. Running offensive plays like a fast break in basketball was a daunting challenge for any player, but especially an offensive lineman.

Kelce came back in 2013 and started right where he left off. Despite the devastating injury, Kelce was still able to make the blocks in space that he made in the past. Running back LeSean McCoy lead the NFL with 1,607 rushing yards, thanks in large part to Kelce's outstanding play. The Eagles scored a team-record 442 points and gained 6,676 total yards on offense. The team honored Kelce's comeback by naming him their Ed Block Courage Award winner. He was also named the top center in the NFL by Pro Football Focus.

As he was entering the final season of his four-year rookie deal, Philadelphia rewarded Kelce with a six-year, $37.5 million contract extension, that included $13 million guaranteed. Despite undergoing hernia surgery and missing four games, Kelce was named to his first Pro Bowl in 2014.

The 2015 season was more of the same for Kelce. He started all 16 games for Philadelphia. The Eagles struggled in their final season under Kelly, going 6 – 9 before he was fired. Once Kelly was gone, Doug Pederson was brought in to replace him. Pederson brought a more traditional West Coast offense with him.

Kelce was still required to make the calls on the line but didn't have to do so at the lightning quick speed that Kelly required. The 2016 season was a tough one for Kelce. He initially found himself struggling against some of the big defensive tackles such as Danny Shelton then of the Cleveland Browns and Eddie Goldman of the Chicago Bears. The Eagles still held on to win both games.

Rookie quarterback Carson Wentz got off to a hot start after being rushed into duty as a starter. Former Eagles offensive coordinator Frank Reich pointed out how Kelce was a key piece in Wentz being able to settle into the starter role. "I can't begin to tell you how much of a benefit it is for Carson to have Jason Kelce as his center," Reich said after their win over the Bears. "Those two are on the same page, and Carson is extremely confident that Kelce is going to get the right things communicated up front."

In a more pro-style offense, the center is leaned upon to call out the changes in protection and help identify the defense. According to Reich, Kelce has done a great job of keeping things in order before the snap. "The guy is brilliant in pass protection calls and scheme," Reich said. "He has this confidence about him that I think sets the tone for what we do in protection."

While the praise was coming from his offensive coordinator, Kelce felt he needed to step his game up. His idea for doing so meant getting back to the fundamental techniques that he relied upon in his journey to one of the top centers in the league. Since he wasn't the biggest center, Kelce always had to rely on quickness and leverage to go against some of the NFL's larger defensive tackles.

"As far as the size, he's probably not the biggest guy in the world, but he gets by with his smarts and athleticism. He's a very tough individual," head coach Doug Pederson said.

The injury bug got Kelce once again in 2016. He had an issue with plantar fasciitis starting in October. It caused him to miss practice time, but he still managed to play in every game.

Carson Wentz and Kelce ran into some fumbling issues during the season. A lot of media types and fans wanted to blame Kelce, but Doug Pederson said the fumbles were on both accounts. "A little bit center, a lot of it quarterback actually. It's something as a quarterback, again, he [Carson Wentz] just took his eyes off the ball, was looking at his read, whether it was a defensive line or a linebacker, and just didn't secure the football," Pederson said. "Kelce wasn't perfect. The balls were off to the right just a touch, and so it was a little bit of the center, a little bit more of the quarterback just taking his eyes off the ball."

Wentz admitted to taking his eye off the ball when it was snapped because he was trying to read the defense. Opposing defenses challenged Wentz by sending blitzes against him. The Eagles did an excellent job against the blitz, which was the result of Wentz being able to pick it up early. That came from getting an early read on it, which is why there were times that he took his eyes off the ball.

Kelce also had a key role in Philadelphia's excellence against the blitz. Pederson credited his center with helping Wentz during weekly preparation. He called Kelce the glue of the offensive line, crediting him with making all of the calls. "I think as a rookie quarterback, you rely on him as a veteran center to make some of the calls in the protection," Pederson explained. "The one thing with Carson [Wentz], he and Jason [Kelce] do a great job during the week of watching film together so that they're making the same calls together and they see the same thing. So, they've been on the same page that way, which is unique to have a rookie quarterback and a veteran center to be as tight as they are in making these calls during the game."

Although he struggled at points in the season, the Eagles Week Ten game against the Falcons was somewhat of a redemption game for Kelce. Kelce was very critical of his previous performance when he spoke to the media during the week leading up to game day. He felt he needed to play better if he wanted to remain the starter.

Philadelphia gained 208 yards on the ground in a 24 – 15 win over the Falcons. Kelce was able to once again get out in space and make blocks freeing the likes of running back Ryan Mathews and rookie Wendell Smallwood.

Kelce was named to the Pro Bowl in 2016, but still felt he had to improve his play the following year. He was an alternate addition after Falcons center Alex Mack was pulled from the roster since Atlanta was headed to Super Bowl LI.

For Kelce, the ultimate goal was to make himself exempt from a Pro Bowl in 2017 by making it to Super Bowl LII. Entering the 2017 season, there were reports that Philadelphia was going to move on from Kelce.

With a $6.2 million cap figure, Executive VP of football operations Howie Roseman had a decision to make. Quarterback Carson Wentz made it clear where he stood regarding Kelce.

"Yeah, I love Kelce. I can't say enough about him," Wentz said when asked about the center on SportsRadio 94WIP FM. "He did a great job physically, but mentally he was just great for me to really bounce ideas off of. He and I together were calling the protections and getting things dialed in. He was a really good guy for me to have, especially year one."

Roseman stressed the need to refrain from being shortsighted and move on from Kelce without having a definitive person to replace him. It made sense. They had invested heavily in the offensive line, and Kelce was the nucleus. Offensive line coach Jeff Stoutland said that he might have put too much on Kelce which resulted in some of the struggles in 2016.

"To be fair to Kelce, I asked him last year to do a whole bunch," said Stoutland. "I think I asked him to do a little bit too much. I think that kind of diluted a little bit of his ability—his production level—a little bit to be honest. That's on me. This year we tightened it up a little bit and put him in better positions to be productive and successful. But I always had tremendous regard for Jason Kelce and his ability to play center in this league, trust me."

There were things that Kelce wanted to fix as far as technique was concerned. He more than did that the following season. They approached the year with a game plan.

"We really looked hard at a lot of the technique things. Stout [Eagles OL coach Jeff Stoutland] has been very critical, and I don't know if it's when you're younger you get away with things because you're a little bit more athletic and a little bit stronger, but I started to lose track of some of the fundamentals that allowed me to play at a high level."

Kelce explained how his hands were out of place at times. They were on the outside instead of inside on the numbers which would have allowed him to drive defenders.

"If you look at a couple games early last year it seems like I always have my hands outside. If you're heavier you can get away with that, but when you're already undersized, and you're losing that aspect of power, you're losing the leverage game, you're going to struggle. Bad technique as well as being undersized is a bad recipe for an offensive lineman," Kelce said.

The 2017 season was filled with solid performances by the Eagles offense. Kelce and Wentz minimized the botched snaps. Whenever Doug Pederson dialed up their outside zone runs, it was Kelce on the move getting out in front of the running back and clearing the way. Kelce improved immensely as he showed that he was still capable of being a top center in the league.

The Kelce family achieved a milestone when the Eagles hit the road to face the Kanas City Chiefs in Week Two of the 2017 season. Chiefs tight end Travis Kelce is Jason's younger brother. He couldn't wait to compete on the same field as his brother. The competition they had growing up helped fuel Travis's path to the NFL.

"Literally everything you could think of, we turned into some sort of game, some sort of competition," Travis said before the game. "Every single day was a new challenge trying to beat my brother in anything. So, it definitely made me an athlete, and the competitive player I am today."

Kanas City came emerged as the winner of the game, but it would be Jason that had the last laugh at the end of the season. Philadelphia's rushing attack showed great improvement. They finished the year with the NFL's fourth-ranked rushing attack, averaging 123.3 yards per game.

Kelce was named a first-team All-Pro but was not voted to the Pro Bowl. Former offensive coordinator Frank Reich was dumbfounded by the omission. "I don't think there's anybody better. I mean, I understand there's a lot of great players in this league," offensive coordinator Frank Reich said about Kelce. "When it comes to a center pulling, getting on the edge, doing the things that Kelce does, he has unique and rare athleticism for a player at his position, and he utilizes that."

Doug Pederson gave Kelce credit for fighting through the tough times in 2016 and emerging as a better player. There was no way Kelce shouldn't have been a Pro Bowl player in his coach's mind. "He's just sort of settled in and is playing. This year he's just let everything go by the wayside and play. He's let loose and played within his skill set and has done a good job. He's been nicked up but continues to play at a high level. He's definitely deserving of that honor [Pro Bowl]," Pederson said.

Kelce thought it was ironic that his past Pro Bowl selections came in years that he felt he really struggled. "Both the years that I went, I think were two of the worst years I've probably had," Kelce said with a smile at his locker on Wednesday. "The one year I had sports hernia surgery and missed about four games. I was pretty hobbled when I came back. Last year was probably the worst year of my career. It's pretty ironic that the two years that I went, I don't think I deserved to be going."

The bigger goal for everyone was to get to the Super Bowl. As they dominated opponents on game day, they still didn't get the respect they deserved. Despite having the best record in the NFL and the top seed in the NFC, the Eagles were still not picked to beat the Falcons in the divisional round of the playoffs at Lincoln Financial Field.

Even after holding on to beat Atlanta and advancing to the NFC Championship game, Philadelphia was not favored to be the Minnesota Vikings at home. Being the underdog was something the team adopted as a mantra during their Super Bowl run.

Going against the New England Patriots was portrayed as an impossible mission, but the Eagles were up for the task. After pulling off the improbable 41-33 win and becoming Super Bowl champions, Kelce opened up about his journey. "The last two weeks after we won I found myself in the shower crying, dreaming about this moment. You work so hard your whole life to get here. Everything cumulates," Kelce said from the podium after the Super Bowl. "I can't help but think of a quote that my grandfather gave me from Calvin Coolidge. He gave me the quote when I was eighteen years old, not given a scholarship to play at any Division I university.

"My father and mother told me to stay after my dreams," Kelce continued as he fought back tears. "I have officially accomplished the best thing in this sport with a group of guys that mean the world to me. The resiliency of this team, when you really sit back and think. A lot of you guys picked us to finish dead last in the NFC East. As the season went along, nobody gave us any inclination that we were the best team in the

NFL. We were able to overcome everything and keep moving forward, I can't help but be a little emotional."

Kelce thanked the Eagles as an organization for sticking with him. He was appreciative of the assistance he got from coach Stoutland and mentioned how he had outstanding teammates on the offensive line that made his job easier. There was a point in 2016 when Kelce really questioned whether or not he belonged in the NFL. He thought maybe he didn't have it anymore. That was over a year ago. A lot can change in a year. Now here he was, rated as one of the best centers in the NFL and a Super Bowl champion.

Lane Johnson Came Back and Showed He Can Be One of the Best

Eagles right tackle Lane Johnson is never afraid to speak his mind. Before the season started, Johnson promised to buy Bud Light for the city of Philadelphia if the Eagles won the Super Bowl. Back when Johnson made that statement, he was out to show that he can be a top player after missing 10 games due to suspension in 2016. Johnson returned from his suspension and kicked butt in the final two games of the season.

He looked to continue where he left off when the 2017 season started. There was a certain focus from Johnson that stood out to his coaching staff. "He's off the chart right now. I think he just made his mind up that he wants to be a dominating player. From the time he walks in until the time he leaves here, it's all business for Lane. Lane's a worker, man. He's always had that in him, but I think it's at a different level right now," offensive line coach Jeff Stoutland said.

Johnson's path to one of the most dominant offensive tackles in the game was rather unique. The former All-State honorable mention quarterback from Groveton High School in Texas took the junior college route, landing at Kilgore College in East Texas.

While at Kilgore, Johnson played quarterback and tight end. After one season at Kilgore, Johnson transferred to Oklahoma. He spent the 2009 season as a redshirt then played tight end and defensive end in 2010.

In 2011, the decision was made to switch Johnson to offensive tackle. A different switch in the past had worked for Oklahoma head coach Bob Stoops. "It was coach Stoops that wanted to move me to tackle. I think it was Mark Mangino who was at Kansas that got into his ear. He told Bob to move Jammal Brown from defensive tackle to offensive tackle.

Brown went in the first round [number 13 overall in the 2005 NFL Draft]," Johnson explained.

They saw how big and athletic Johnson was and figured the move would be successful. Johnson took advantage of his basketball past which helped him make the transition. "Years of basketball helped me as far as the footwork. Going from quarterback to tight end, the physical part, that was the toughest during my redshirt year at Oklahoma," Johnson said. "Getting the steps, getting my hands right, that's something I never had to do. Mirroring people—that came naturally to me."

Once Johnson moved to tackle, his career took off at Oklahoma. He started 12 of 13 games at right tackle as a junior. The following year he switched to left tackle and was named a third-team All-American.

Johnson continued his excellence as a senior when he went to Mobile, Alabama to take part in the Senior Bowl in 2013. During the practice week, Johnson impressed scouts as a member of the South team, which was coached by former Detroit Lions head coach Jim Schwartz.

Bucky Brooks of NFL.com shared some of his notes on Johnson after watching him in practice. "Johnson has demonstrated impressive footwork, balance, and body control while snuffing out pass rushers in drills. In one-on-one drills, Johnson's capacity to anchor and redirect rushers has earned him high marks from scouts closely monitoring his game," Brooks said.

Johnson was named the Senior Bowl's Most Outstanding Lineman. The meteoric rise for Johnson was heightened after an awesome display at the NFL Combine in Indianapolis. He completed all of the combine drills and finished first in the vertical jump (34 inches) and second amongst all offensive linemen in the 40-yard dash (4.72 seconds) and broad jump (nine feet, ten inches).

The Eagles selected Johnson with the fourth overall pick in the 2013 NFL Draft. Although he was selected behind Eric Fisher (number one overall to Chiefs) and Luke Joeckel (number two overall to Jaguars), Johnson proved to be the best of the group.

Philadelphia had future Hall of Fame left tackle Jason Peters in place on the left side, so Johnson had to play right tackle like he did his junior year. During training camp, Johnson competed with Dennis Kelly for the starting spot and was named the starter after Kelly had to undergo back surgery. Johnson started all 16 games as a rookie for an Eagles team that went 10 – 6 and captured the NFC East Division title. The season ended on a low note when Philadelphia lost to the New Orleans Saints in the first round of the playoffs.

The 2014 season got off to a rough start for Johnson when it was reported that he tested positive for a performance-enhancing drug in June. He had to sit out the first four games due to a league-imposed suspension. Johnson was on a mission to prove his worth when he came back. He only allowed one sack in the remaining 12 games. Johnson showed that he can be an elite tackle without the added assistance of PEDs. Despite dealing with various injuries, Johnson started all 16 games in 2015. He showed his versatility when he flipped over to left tackle for two games that Jason Peters missed due to a back injury.

Head coach Chip Kelly was fired after going 6 – 9 that season. The new regime under Doug Pederson was convinced that Johnson should be one of the core players the Eagles would build around. Entering the fourth year of his rookie deal, Johnson signed a six-year, $63 million extension with $35.5 million guaranteed. Johnson and Jason Peters were going to be the bookend tackles for years to come.

In August it was reported that Johnson was facing a 10-game suspension as a result of testing positive for performance-enhancing drugs for the second time. Johnson told Fox Sports's Jay Glazer that he had taken an amino acid supplement that was approved, but it tested positive for a peptide which is a compound of amino acids. Johnson claimed he purchased a supplement online that was approved by the NFLPA phone app, Aegis Shield. The amino acid supplement was supposedly approved by the NFL Players Association.

When he tested positive the first time back in 2014, Johnson took the blame. This time around was an honest mistake according to Johnson. "The first time, I knew I was at fault. There's no worse feeling than having to go through this again. This is something that I definitely wanted to avoid. It's nothing I ever wanted to be a part of again. I learned my lesson," Johnson said in August 2016. "I want that to be clear, that the NFLPA does not stand up for players. They don't check the supplements. They give us an app, and then when you call them and ask them if you test positive for something they approve, it doesn't matter. That's all I got to say about that."

The player's association fought back saying they don't approve supplements. They also said players should be aware that not all ingredients in the supplement are listed on the label.

Despite the looming suspension, Johnson continued to take part in training camp but with the second-team offense. The fourth-year tackle has vowed to never take supplements again. "Seriously, I don't want to have to go through this again," Johnson said. "Unless something changes—the policy—I don't trust anything. I can't risk it. If it happens again, I miss two years, and I'm just not going to risk that happening. I'm not taking any chances. Food and water. That's all I'm going to put in my system. No supplements, no powders, nothing. Look in everybody's locker. Everybody's got 'em. But you just don't know what's really in them."

The suspension didn't stop Johnson from starting the season as the right tackle. Somehow he managed to focus on football as he prepared for the season. Pederson kept him as the starter. "Until I get further word from the league office, he goes in as my starting right tackle," Pederson said after the final preseason game. "Going forward, he [Johnson] goes in as our right tackle, and we'll move Allen [Barbre] back to left guard."

The suspension was upheld in October after an appeal by Johnson. With Johnson in the starting lineup, the Eagles proceeded to start the season 3 – 0. Johnson began serving his suspension after the bye week. Using a patchwork offensive line with rookie Halipoulivaati Vaita at right tackle, Philadelphia only won two of their next eleven games.

When Johnson came back, he was on a mission much like he was in 2014. The energy and excitement that he had was something his coaches and teammates noticed. Johnson blocked like a possessed man when he was back in the lineup. He pulled to the outside on two occasions and took out a couple of defenders leading to long runs by the backs.

"First play of the game, you know he just kind of picked up where he left off. He did a great job on that first play, and he was out running," coach Doug Pederson said at his postgame press conference.

The Eagles won the following week against the Dallas Cowboys to finish on a high with a two-game winning streak. Things were about to get exciting for Johnson and the Eagles in 2017.

Johnson got some reps at left tackle during the spring just in case he had to switch sides due to injury or any unforeseen circumstance. It was a refresher course for the veteran offensive lineman. "I got drafted playing left tackle. It's really just getting the reps. The deal was to get me the reps," Johnson said at his locker after practice on Thursday. "JP [Jason Peters] isn't here, so I get the reps, and whenever I do go to left tackle, it won't be five or six years of not playing it then getting in. It's money in the bank I'd say."

Player Spotlight: The Offensive Line

Before the season, Johnson wrote an entry for the *Player's Tribune*. He talked about how last year helped him become a more focused player and how it was terrible watching his team lose knowing he could be out there helping them. In summary, Johnson said, "In other words, this situation has lit a fire under my ass."

He also made a proclamation that his team will start the season off with a bang and keep going from there.

"Let me tell you what's going to happen in a couple of weeks," Johnson said. "This team is going to go down to D.C. and whup some ass against the Redskins. We're going to surprise some people. That's where the momentum is going to begin, and then the hype train is just going to get bigger as the league realizes that the Eagles are back."

The Eagles opened with a win over the Washington Redskins followed by a loss to the Kansas City Chiefs. After that, they proceeded to win the next nine games. Johnson suffered a concussion in Week Five against the Arizona Cardinals and was taken out of the game in the third quarter. He missed the following week against the Carolina Panthers before returning in Week Seven against the Redskins.

Left tackle Jason Peters suffered torn ligaments in his knee against the Redskins and was done for the year. There was some thought to moving Johnson to left tackle, but Doug Pederson made a wise decision to keep Johnson on the right side where he was already excelling.

Now the spotlight was on Johnson to lead the offensive line. He had already been making his mark as one of the top tackles in football. This was only going to allow him to further entrench himself among the elite. Johnson faced the ultimate test a couple of weeks later when Philadelphia hosted outside linebacker Von Miller and the Denver Broncos. Miller is one of the NFL's top pass rushers. It was up to Johnson to neutralize him.

Miller was unable to register a sack against Johnson and was no factor in the game. One of Johnson's blocks against Miller became a highlight of the season. He managed to execute a hit on the All-Pro pass rusher that would make the pro-wrestling world proud.

"I acted like I was getting a pass set to get him up the field. I clubbed him when he was trying to spin inside of me, and I timed it just right. It looked a lot better than what it was," Johnson said as he laughed while describing the play on NFL Network's top 100 players show.

Miller, DeMarcus Lawrence, Joey Bosa, Melvin Ingram—one by one they all lined up against Johnson and each of them were neutralized.

The Eagles were not getting the respect they felt they deserved even though they dominated their opponents. Talking heads continued to deny them the title of being the top team in the NFC. Johnson was not too fond of that, and he's never afraid to speak his mind. He appeared on FS1's "First Things First" to chat with co-host Nick Wright who was one of the main Eagles doubters.

"Just see who we've gone against. And I think, you know, we have six more games left to play so we can just keep proving you wrong," Johnson said. "I mean, I think people were like 'It's too good to be true.' And that's fine and dandy, but we are who we are, and we're confident in what we're doing."

The doubts only increased when Carson Wentz was lost for the season against the Los Angeles Rams. Suddenly everyone felt the year was over for the Eagles without Wentz.

"What bothered me is we were 12 – 2, and we got treated like we were the Browns. I don't like it, but I think it's a good motivator," Johnson said. "We come in, and Nick Foles is the new quarterback. He's not putting up 400 yards passing, so people panic."

Even though there were doubts about Philadelphia being the NFL's top team, there was little dispute as to who the league's top right tackle was. Johnson received a Pro Bowl nomination and was named a first-team All-Pro.

Having held his own against a series of elite pass rushers in the regular season prove that Johnson deserved to be mentioned as one of the best tackles. He got to prove it even further in the divisional round of the playoffs against Vic Beasley and the Atlanta Falcons. Johnson jokingly asked if Godzilla was going to be his next opponent.

Atlanta was the number six seed in the playoffs, but they still were favored to beat the number one seeded Eagles. The disrespect infuriated Johnson, but he used it as fuel for his fire. "I'd rather have people not write good things. I think that's the best motivator there is. Ultimately, it's all up to us, but a lot of what you guys do motivates guys. It motivates me, it motivates a lot of guys in here," Johnson said.

After winning the playoff matchup with the Falcons, Johnson and some of his teammates walked off the field with a dog mask on to mock their status as underdogs. Johnson even did his postgame interviews at his locker wearing a dog mask.

Player Spotlight: The Offensive Line

The concept took off, so Johnson found a way to use it to help serve the community. He sold underdog shirts on his website with the proceeds going to a good cause. "We figured it'd be a good way to raise money for the schools," Johnson said. "It's going to the Philadelphia School District. It's not going to one school. It's going to be spread out. We got it set up with the mayor."

Next up for the Eagles were the Minnesota Vikings in a battle for the right to play in Super Bowl LII. When Johnson came out during pregame introductions, he held up a number 71 jersey in a tribute to Jason Peters. "He was a special part of the team," Johnson said after the game. "Just a guy who means so much to the team and would kill to be out there. I wanted to do him service for what he is."

The tone was set, and Philadelphia put a serious beatdown on the Vikings, winning the game 38 – 7. Earlier that day, the New England Patriots beat the Jacksonville Jaguars to punch their ticket to the Super Bowl.

Never one to back down from a challenge, Johnson turned his sights on the next opponent. "Hey, Tom Brady. Pretty boy Tom Brady," Johnson said when asked about Philadelphia's opponent in Super Bowl LII. "He's the best quarterback of all time, so [there's] nothing I'd like to do more than dethrone that guy. For what they did to us in [the] 2004 [season], to get payback, there would be nothing sweeter than that. I remember watching that game when I was fourteen years old. I was hoping the Eagles would win. Just coming up short, you could feel the pain, and you could also feel the passion of what this city wants. And we're here, so it's right at our fingertips."

Super Bowl media week for Johnson was a blast. He was always one of the players that drew the most attention at his podium. On opening night, Johnson wore a funny hat and John Lennon-like sunglasses while he was at the podium. Johnson fielded plenty of questions about his Patriots comments. He continued to stick by his words.

When game time arrived, it was all business for Johnson and the Eagles on the field. The infamous play affectionately known as 'The Philly Special' happened on Johnson's side of the field. It was a crucial play in their 41 – 33 victory over the Patriots.

After the game, Johnson talked about how important it was to bring a Lombardi Trophy home for the city of Philadelphia. "Ever since I've gotten into this town all we've talked about is winning the Super Bowl. They got close in 2004, had some great teams, lot of ups and downs, this championship means more to the city than those other world championships means to others," Johnson said. "It's what they've been talking about there since 1960. They love their sports, it's like a religion. Come parade time, who knows what's going to happen. The streets are already flooded—a lot of chaos, lots of pandemonium. I'm going to love every second of it."

There was one little detail that was left out from the summertime. Johnson had promised to give Bud Light to everyone in Philadelphia if they won a championship. It was time to pay up. Bud Light got in on the promise as well. They provided free beer to the fans during the Super Bowl parade.

On the day of the parade, we invite all fans 21+ to join us in raising the Kingdom's favorite light lager in celebration of the big win. Look for Bud Light reps at multiple taverns along the parade route where we will buy fans one Bud Light. Congrats, Philadelphia! And please enjoy responsibly!

Philly Philly!

Johnson was one of the driving forces for the Eagles' Super Bowl run. His willingness to speak his mind to the media and back it up on the field served as a catalyst for the team.

As he looked back on the season during OTAs the following spring, Johnson shared the biggest lesson he pulled from the Super Bowl run. "Be confident, be yourself. I am not trying to be nobody else. I made all of those statements before the season. Everybody was talking about the Redskins and people looking at me coming off the suspension, 'What can this guy do?' I showed them what I could do, and it kept on developing into a Super Bowl team," Johnson explained. "I think it's all about the mindset. You need leaders that can be bold. Not to be cocky or arrogant, but I think we are going to press the envelope and maximize what we have here. If we do that we will win a lot of ball games."

Brandon Brooks Found Himself in Philly

After four seasons with the Houston Texans, right guard Brandon Brooks signed a five-year contract worth $50 million that included an $11 million signing bonus and $21 million guaranteed. Along with former Baltimore Ravens guard Kelechi Osemele and former San Francisco 49ers guard Alex Boone, Brooks was one of the top three guards to hit free agency in 2016.

Other teams were interested in acquiring his services. However, Brooks knew Philadelphia was where he wanted to play because of the players already on the offensive line as well as the way they came after him from the start of the free agency period.

"The biggest thing for me was when things opened up on Monday, just from the get-go, the Eagles let me know that I was their guy. I felt wanted," Brooks said. "Players on the team—Peters, Kelce, Lane—they all texted me saying to come here, and that we have an opportunity to build something great."

"Lane [Johnson] is one of the best young right tackles in the league. Kelce has been doing this for a long time. He is one of the best pulling centers I have ever seen," Brooks said. "I really want to learn from Kelce. He was the first or second guy to text me. I want him to take me under his wing, along with Peters, to help me take my game to the next level."

Brooks wasn't always the player that everyone wanted. Playing for Riverside University High School in Milwaukee, Brooks helped his school capture a city championship and an appearance in the 2006 state semifinals.

Brooks ended up at Miami of Ohio University where he was a four-year starter after a redshirting in 2007. He played mostly as a guard except of 2010 when he missed part of the season due to injury and played left tackle for two games. After his senior season, he set his sights on the NFL but was not invited to the 2012 NFL Combine. That didn't stop the Texans from selecting Brooks in the third round (number 76 overall) of the 2012 NFL Draft.

Under head coach Gary Kubiak, Houston utilized a zone scheme that employed more athletic offensive linemen. Brooks was a perfect match for their scheme but so was fellow rookie Ben Jones, a 2012 fourth-round pick out of Georgia.

Jones started 10 games in 2012 with Brooks being active over the last six. Both rookies surpassed veteran guard Antoine Caldwell after he started the first six games. Brooks became the starter at right guard in 2013 and held the position through the 2015 season. He only missed three games over his three seasons as a starter for the Texans.

One of the games he missed came in December 2015. Brooks rode on the team bus to the stadium for their game against the Buffalo Bills thinking he'd be able to shake the pain. He kept sweating and vomiting, so the Texans medical staff tried to give him fluids.

Brooks was taken to the hospital with stomach pains and remained at Erie County Medical Center as the Texans made their trip back to Houston after the game. He was later diagnosed with stomach ulcers. The stomach issues resurfaced during Brooks's first season with the Eagles in 2016. Brooks was a surprise scratch from the Eagles lineup before their Week

Twelve Monday Night Football game against the Green Bay Packers. He was taken to the hospital and released the following morning after having the issues with nausea. Brooks returned to the first practice after being released from the hospital.

He recounted what happened leading up to him being taken to the hospital. "I woke up at five a.m. on the dot because my stomach was doing backflips and I started throwing up uncontrollably," Brooks said at his locker. "I didn't stop until later on that night. I went to the hospital. It was just a stomach bug that was going around. They gave me an IV and other medications to try and stop me up. I didn't feel better until nine p.m."

Brooks wouldn't say what he ate but said it was just the regular stuff they serve at the hotel the night before the game. He never made it to the stadium for the game.

The following week seemed like everything was all right. Brooks traveled with the team to Cincinnati for their game against the Bengals and played without any issues. Things didn't go so smoothly after the Bengals game. Nausea and vomiting got the best of Brooks once again. He was not activated for their game against the Washington Redskins.

At that point, it was more important to get to the bottom of the issues that were causing Brooks's illness. The medical staff couldn't quite put a finger on what was causing it initially, but soon discovered that Brooks had anxiety issues.

"I found out recently that I have an anxiety condition," Brooks said at his locker. "It's not nervousness or fear of the game. I have an obsession with the game. It's an unhealthy obsession right now. I love this organization. They have been great and have supported me with this. I will make it through. It's nothing that I am ashamed of. I own it."

Brooks was given the option to keep his condition private, but he chose to reveal the truth. He wanted to be clear that he was not nervous or intimidated by football. Brooks said he loves the game but obsesses over it to the point that it causes the anxiety attacks on game day. Brooks managed to stay clear of any pregame anxiety attacks over the final three games of the season. He had to find a way to keep them from happening in the future as well.

Discovering the reason for his anxiety attacks was the first step. Taking measures to cope with it was next. Brooks sought counseling and developed ways to relax when he felt the anxiety rising within him.

Player Spotlight: The Offensive Line

"I started talking to a therapist in getting to the root of why I looked at football and mistakes so intensely, and why I thought to a certain degree that if I made a mistake, my whole world would come crashing down," Brooks said. "I'm light years ahead of where I was in regards to that thought process. I can say that it's something that's behind me. I can't say I still don't get the butterflies, but it's nowhere near the extreme of where I'll miss a game because I'm physically ill. I think those days are behind me. I look forward to being out there every Sunday, barring injury, and going from there."

It is unusual for an offensive lineman to be in the spotlight, but Brooks became a more well-known player because of his open approach to his bout with anxiety issues.

During the offseason, Brooks spoke to kids at Southern Elementary School in New Castle, Delaware. He got to meet a young man who had a similar fight with anxiety issues. "He wanted to say something to me, but he really couldn't; he was almost locked up," said Brooks. "Being able to sit there and talk to him to let him know that I went through the same thing or some type of version of it I think really helped him out."

"To go and sit next to him and tell him that I fight the same demons, that hit here for me," Brooks said as he pointed to his heart. "To have someone in my position and reach out to him, hopefully, that will make an impact in his life. I plan to go back and talk to him to help him out. I told him that it was no different for me."

Eagles fans took to Brooks after his first season in Philadelphia. One even invited Brooks to attend his wedding. The fan happened to also be a graduate of Miami of Ohio, which is Brooks's alma mater. Brooks took the fan up on his offer and attended the wedding.

"A lot of times we, as athletes, get put on this pedestal, and we think we are better than someone else. We are no different. It was really my honor to be invited to the wedding," Brooks said.

Like many of the blue-collar people in the greater Philadelphia area, Brooks is not afraid of putting in extra work. In addition to getting ready for the season, Brooks doubled as an intern with the City of Philadelphia's Department of Finance and Revenue. Before he got to the NFL, Brooks earned a business degree from Miami of Ohio. While in college, Brooks listed economist.com as his favorite website according to the school's program.

Some of the things that were of particular interest to Brooks during his internship were seeing how the city wage tax was structured as well as how the soda tax was applied. Brooks also enjoyed spending time working with the Susquehanna International Group doing equity options research. "I looked through balance sheets, 10Ks, financial analysis, relative analysis to help the traders out. I learned a lot and had a ton of fun," Brooks said with a smile.

The days were long for Brooks during the offseason which is normally a time when players are on vacation in some exotic island or in Europe. Brooks worked his internship from 7:30 a.m. to 4:30 p.m. then went to the NovaCare Complex to work out from 5:30 p.m. to 7:30 p.m. He put the time in for sure. The long hours paid off for Brooks. He and the Eagles got off to a great start in 2017 that was highlighted by a nine-game win streak.

One of Brooks's best plays came on a 46-yard touchdown run by Jay Ajayi against the Denver Broncos. Big number 79 lumbered down the field and got the final block to help Ajayi in the open field. A six-foot, five-inch, 346-pound player is not usually known for his athleticism, but Brandon Brooks showed plenty of athleticism on Ajayi's long touchdown run.

Eagles offensive line coach Jeff Stoutland called Brooks sneaky athletic. Stoutland thought about Brooks's downfield block and smiled during media availability. "It's pretty awesome, then he can stand at the line of scrimmage in a phone booth and knock your face off," Stoutland said. "Brooks has been really consistent all year long. He's playing at a very, very high level. I am just so happy he's our right guard."

Stoutland is proud of how Brooks fought through it and came out on top. "He's a tough guy mentally. To me, he's just a whole different guy right now, every facet of the game," Stoutland said. "Right now, he's feeling good about where he's at. He's enjoying the game right now, I know that."

Stoutland wasn't the only person that saw how well Brooks played in 2017. He was named to the Pro Bowl for the first time in his career. Making the Pro Bowl was a goal for Brooks, but he had a bigger goal, which was to play in all 16 games. That's exactly what he did. Doing so showed that he had truly put his anxiety issues behind him.

Not everyone supported Brooks when he had a low point the previous year. Brooks didn't forget that. "When I was going through the anxiety stuff, not everybody had my back. But at the same time, it's interesting to me now, the Pro Bowl is here, so the same people who didn't support me are here to pat me on the back. Let it be understood that, although you forgive, you never forget," Brooks said.

As the Eagles worked their way towards the playoffs, Brooks continued his excellent play. Along with the rest of the offensive line, Brooks helped pave the way for one of the most balanced offenses in the NFL. They powered through the Falcons and Vikings *en route* to Super Bowl LII. It was the biggest stage a professional football player could be on. All of the attention and media coverage was now focused on two teams.

That surely couldn't be good for someone who fights anxiety right? Brooks handled media week like a seasoned veteran. The bright lights and hype of media week didn't bother him. He looked back at how he opened up about his issues with anxiety the previous year and embraced it.

Knowing the media would be searching for answers when he missed two games in three weeks, the Eagles' PR department gave Brooks two avenues. He could either be honest and tell what was going on or give an excuse. "At that point, I didn't have anything to hide. I didn't want to lie about it. I was comfortable with myself knowing what it was. People wanted me to tell the truth, but there also were some who didn't want me to say anything," Brooks said.

Other players had similar issues and shared them with Brooks. He hoped the way he shared his story would help others understand that football players are people too. "In a game where you are looked at as a modern day gladiator, and nothing is supposed to affect you, people think you are not supposed to have emotions," Brooks said during media availability. "I asked for help. I internalize things so much it started eating me from the inside out."

Brooks's pursuit of perfection on the football field and in life caused him to view any type of mistake as the end of the world. A mistake in the Super Bowl would seem like that to some players. It's a game that will be watched by the whole world.

For someone like Brooks, it was all about staying ahead of the issue.

"Seeing signs of it coming on when it does and dealing with it has been good. I know how to control it," Brooks explained. "I know why it's going on. Even this week with it being the Super Bowl, the biggest game of my life, I have a little anxiety, but it's totally under control. I know as the game gets closer it will come on for sure, but I will be fine."

The game took place, and Brooks lined up at his normal right guard position to protect quarterback Nick Foles as well as open up holes for the running backs. He played every offensive snap for Philadelphia as they defeated the New England Patriots to win the city's first Super Bowl.

He showed how a person can go through some dark times but fight through them and bounce back like a champion. Each of the Eagles offensive linemen were underdogs in some way.

That's how the team was. No one expected the Eagles to win it all. They weren't picked to win in their own stadium despite being the top seed in their conference. None of that mattered to them. After only two seasons, Doug Pederson led the Eagles to a position where they could hoist the Lombardi Trophy.

They embraced the underdog role. As Jason Kelce said during his epic speech after the parade, "We were all hungry dogs, and hungry dogs run faster!"

Player Spotlight: Mychal Kendricks

Eagles linebacker Mychal Kendricks's path to Super Bowl champion was a long, difficult road. He has gone from the player everyone loved to one everyone wanted to criticize and back.

Kendricks is one of the longest-tenured players on the team. He is one of a handful of players whose time in Philadelphia dates back to the days of former head coach Andy Reid. It seemed like every year there were questions about whether or not he would be back with the Eagles the following season. Despite all of that, Kendricks persevered and can now add world champion to his list of accomplishments.

In the Beginning

Originally selected in the second round (number 46 overall) of the 2012 NFL Draft, Kendricks has played for three Eagles head coaches. As a senior in 2011, Kendricks was the Pac-12 Defensive Player of the Year after recording 106 tackles, three sacks, and two interceptions. Being selected by the Eagles had a special meaning to Kendricks. His father, Marvin Kendricks, was on the Eagles Training Camp roster in 1972. While Mychal went to Cal years later, his father played for UCLA where he was the school's leading rusher in 1970 and 1971.

"My dad was so happy the day I got drafted here because the Eagles were his team," Kendricks told the Eagles team site. "He followed them all the time when I was growing up. It was a dream come true for the both of us."

Kendricks went into organized team activities as the starting strongside linebacker after signing a four-year, $4.44 million contract that included $2.60 million guaranteed and a signing bonus of $1.67 million. He finished his rookie season in 2012 with 75 combined tackles, nine pass breakups, and a sack in 15 games. Of his 75 tackles, 58 of them were solo tackles.

Kendricks showed the elite athleticism that opened so many eyes at the 2012 NFL Combine. The lightning-quick speed (4.47 seconds in the 40-yard dash), cat-like quickness (4.14 short shuttle), and explosiveness (39.5 inch vertical, 10.7-foot broad jump) were all on display as Kendricks flowed to football.

It seemed like there was a bright future ahead for Kendricks after his promising rookie year.

Changing of the Guard

Reid was let go by the Eagles after finishing at the bottom of the NFC East division with a 4 – 12 record. Former Oregon coach Chip Kelly was hired to be Reid's replacement. Kelly hired Billy Davis to be his defensive coordinator. Davis brought the 3 – 4 defense with him which meant a change of position was for Kendricks. The new defense had Kendricks moving to inside linebacker and called for the defensive front to occupy gaps allowing Kendricks and veteran linebacker DeMeco Ryans to have a clear path to chase down running backs.

"I enjoy pushing myself and seeing what I can accomplish, so to come off the first year, I did some good things and understand there are things I need to improve," Kendricks told the Eagles team site before the 2013 season. "I've really enjoyed the [new] defense. It's fast, and it's a lot different from what we ran last year. We have to make more plays and force more turnovers and get to the quarterback. I look at it like I want to be the one to make those plays. My goal is to take my game to a new level."

Kendricks became a fan favorite in Philadelphia. He even had his own photo cutout erected in JFK Plaza next to the LOVE statue before the season. The second-year linebacker got off to a tremendous start in 2014. For the first time in his career, Kendricks racked up 10 tackles in the season opener against the Washington Redskins. He notched his first interception in Week Five of his second season when he picked off a pass thrown by New York Giants quarterback Eli Manning. Later on in the season, against the Chicago Bears, Kendricks posted his first two-sack game when he took quarterback Jay Cutler down twice.

Kendricks finished the 2013 season with 106 combined tackles, four pass breakups, four sacks, four fumble recoveries, three interceptions, and two forced fumbles in 15 games. He played in 83 percent of the Eagles' defensive snaps in his second season. The Eagles made the playoffs, but Kendricks was not selected to the Pro Bowl despite his impressive numbers. Kendricks had seven tackles in the Eagles' 26 – 24 home loss to the New Orleans Saints in the wildcard playoff game.

Kendricks had his first real bout with an injury in his third season. He left Eagles' Week Two game against the Indianapolis Colts in the third quarter after suffering from an injured calf. The calf injury kept Kendricks from playing in four consecutive games. Later in the season, veteran leader DeMeco Ryans suffered a torn Achilles and was out for the final eight games.

It was time to turn to a different source of leadership. But Kendricks wanted people to understand he had his own unique way of being a leader. "I think that everyone leads different," Kendricks said to the Allentown Morning Call. "I don't think that people know this, but I am a leader in my own way. I have been since the day I got here—in my own way."

He is not the kind of player that will try to rally the troops with yelling or motivational speeches. The "rah-rah, having others circle around him before breaking down the huddle" trait was more of something that Ryans possessed. Kendricks was more of a leader by example. He would instead let his work on the field and in the workouts lead the way.

"The things I do on the field, man," Kendricks mentioned. "You guys see it. It's nothing that needs to be said. It's something that needs to be shown, and I know you guys see it, so it's what I do. Leaders come from all angles on this team."

Kelly urged Kendricks to find his own way of being the leader on defense. "Mychal has just got to be himself, and I think if Mychal tries to be anything different than himself, I don't think that's . . . the formula for success," Kelly said in a press conference before a Week Ten clash with the Carolina Panthers at Lincoln Financial Field. "But I think when you try to become something else or try to say, 'Hey, DeMeco did it this way, so I have to do it that way,' . . . Mychal has got to be Mychal."

Despite playing in 12 games (11 starts), Kendricks finished the 2014 season with 63 solo tackles, 83 combined tackles, four sacks, and three pass breakups. By that point, it was clear that Kendricks was one of the up and coming defensive players in the NFL. With his contract set to expire after the season, Kendricks faced questions about whether or not he would be back in Philadelphia after the 2015 season.

The Eagles had selected linebacker Jordan Hicks in the third-round (number 84 overall) out of Texas in the 2015 NFL Draft. They restructured/extended Ryans's contract by adding one year and lowered his $6.9 million salary cap number for 2015. Philadelphia also acquired linebacker Kiko Alonso from the Buffalo Bills in exchange for well-liked running back LeSean 'Shady' McCoy. Buffalo was looking for a running back, and Philadelphia was looking for a wide receiver. Alonso played for Chip Kelly while the two were at Oregon. He was coming off of a torn ACL that happened while he was working out at Oregon in 2014.

Since Kelly was the primary force behind dealing McCoy, it was pretty clear the player the Eagles got back (Alonso) was going to start. Given the new contract that Kendricks signed, he was for sure going to be the other starting inside linebacker.

When OTAs came around, the Eagles still had not approached Kendricks about a contract extension. Some wondered if Kendricks fit Kelly's 'Big people beat up on little people' approach to measurables for players. Ironically, the two linebackers the Eagles added to the roster (Hicks six-feet, one-inch, 236 pounds) and (Alonso six-feet, three-inches, 239 pounds) were not too different from Kendricks who measured at six-feet, 239 pounds.

"I'm not worried," Kendricks told CSN Philly in June of 2015. "I'm fast. I can get into all the little gaps, all the little holes. I feel like I can cover the field pretty well. Height may be an issue, but I don't worry about all that. I think I am the new prototype."

Having played in both a 4 – 3 and 3 – 4 scheme, Kendricks wouldn't be limited to a particular group of teams if he hit the free agent market. If he was headed to a different team in the future, that wasn't something that would cause Kendricks to be worried.

"There's a saying grass isn't always greener on the other side, and I'm not a future teller so I can't really give you that answer," Kendricks said. "But if I was to be in another position and thrown in as the starter, I would embrace it like I did when I came here."

Kendricks was only 24-years old at the time. He had three solid seasons on his resume. There was little doubt that he would draw interest on the open market. The Eagles realized this and signed Kendricks to a four-year, $29 million contract extension with $16.1 million guaranteed and a signing bonus of $8 million. The deal was set to keep Kendricks in Philadelphia through the 2019 season. It was the Eagles' way of staying ahead of the curve, banking on Kendricks to have another Pro Bowl-caliber season.

"I'm happy for Mych, happy for him and his family," fellow inside linebacker DeMeco Ryans said via CSNPhilly.com. "I'm always happy to see guys getting a deal. Mych is a really exceptional player, one of the best inside linebackers in this league. It's a credit to his work that he's put out on the field. He still has a ways to go, he can still get much better. He knows that. The sky is the limit for Mychal, but I think before it's said and done, he could be the best inside linebacker in this league."

Kendricks wanted the security of a long-term contract before entering the final year of his rookie deal. This way he could focus solely on football. "It feels amazing," Kendricks said on the Eagles' website. "All of the hard work went toward the end goal, which was to reach the second contract and now it's here. It feels really nice. I think security is a big thing, and the fact that it's done early, I can have peace of mind and just go out there and play the game that I love . . . It's a special day."

Years later, the very thing that offered him security ended up being a reason for questions to arise about his status with the team. The 2015 season got off to a rocky start for Kendricks, but he still managed to produce. Kendricks was a part of the competition at inside linebacker that also included Ryans, Alonso, and Hicks. He was able to hold off Hicks and win one of the starting spots. The other position was claimed by Alonso.

Alonso and Kendricks made their debut as a duo in the season opener on the road against the Atlanta Falcons. Kendricks posted 10 tackles in the 24-20 loss to Atlanta. Alonso had the play of the game, a 60-yard interception return for a touchdown. Although the Eagles lost, the pairing of Alonso and Kendricks appeared to have a brilliant future. Unfortunately, the injury bug came calling once again the following week against the Dallas Cowboys.

Alonso suffered a partial tear of the ACL that was repaired in 2014. That was the last time he played a game in an Eagles uniform. Alonso would later be packaged with cornerback Byron Maxwell along with the number 13 pick in the 2016 NFL Draft in exchange for the number eight pick in the 2016 NFL Draft.

Kendricks suffered a hamstring injury in the same game. He missed the following week against the New York Jets but returned for Philadelphia's Week Four clash with the Redskins. He re-aggravated the hamstring injury and missed the next two games. The Eagles got Kendricks back in the lineup in Week Seven just in time for Cam Newton and the Carolina Panthers. Kendricks turned in a stellar performance, racking up eight tackles and a sack. When the season came to a close, the Eagles had a 7 – 9 record. Kendricks finished the season having played 627 snaps (52%) on defense.

Philadelphia fired Kelly before the final game of the season. It was highly unlikely that defensive coordinator Billy Davis would be retained when the next coach took over.

Here We Go Again

Once again, Kendricks was faced with enduring a coaching change which likely meant he would be thrust into another defensive scheme. This time the coaching change would yield a Super Bowl Championship, but it didn't come without more growing pains for Kendricks.

The Eagles hired Doug Pederson to get back to the more personable, family-like atmosphere that Andy Reid once had in place at the NovaCare Complex. Pederson hired Jim Schwartz to be the defensive coordinator. Schwartz brought a 4 – 3 scheme to Philadelphia. Rookie linebacker Jordan Hicks made a splash debut when Kendricks missed time in 2015.

Hicks's first start came in Week Six when he made 10 solo tackles in a 27 — 7 victory over the New York Giants. An outstanding rookie season by Hicks was cut short by a torn pectoral injury that landed Hicks on injured reserve in early November.

Now with a new coaching staff in place, Hicks and Kendricks were installed as starters at middle and weakside linebacker. The 2015 season was the final year for DeMeco Ryans. The long-tenured veteran decided to retire rather than return for the 2016 season. That left a void at linebacker which was filled when the Eagles signed former Bills defender Nigel Bradham. Bradham had played for Schwartz in the past and had a thorough understanding of the playbook. Schwartz's 4 – 3 scheme allowed for Kendricks, Hicks, and Bradham to all be on the field at the same time.

Kendricks was the veteran while Hicks was now the young, hot shot, up-and-coming player. It was just two years ago that Kendricks had played the same role as Hicks and Ryans was the veteran. Suddenly, the Eagles had what appeared to be a well-rounded, complimentary group of linebackers. Unfortunately, things did not get off to the best start for Kendricks.

Coming off a solid season in 2015, Kendricks felt if he got more regular snaps, he could get into a groove. The rotation in 2015 didn't allow him to do so, in Kendricks's opinion. He felt big things were coming in 2016: "I just feel like it was too much hot and cold with all the players rotating in and out,"

Kendricks said in May 2016. "No one was able to get in the flow. It was odd. I didn't feel like I played as good or as much. For the time I was in, I feel like my numbers were okay. But it's hard to be a force or something to reckon with when you're not on the field. . . . I feel like if I stay healthy," he said, "you'll see me in the Pro Bowl."

He missed the first two preseason games in 2016 because he was nursing a hamstring injury. Pederson elected to have Kendricks play into the fourth quarter with the backups during the Eagles' third preseason game in Indianapolis against the Colts.

He gave his reason for Kendricks extensive playing time when he was asked about it after the game. "Because he hasn't played. He hasn't played, and we just want to see him get game and live reps. That's the bottom line," Pederson said matter-of-factly. Pederson also foreshadowed playing time for Kendricks in the last preseason game. "There's a chance he plays because he hasn't played all preseason, and we still want to get him those live reps and get him ready for Cleveland."

The final preseason game is usually reserved for fringe roster players that are playing for their football lives. Most of the starters and established players don't see the field in the fourth preseason game.

However, Kendricks was one of the only projected starters on the field for the last preseason game against the New York Jets. Kendricks played late in that game as well. The plan was to get Kendricks more reps in both base and nickel packages since he missed so many reps during training camp and the other preseason games.

When the 2016 season started, Kendricks remained the starting weakside linebacker. He played 19 snaps on defense and 11 snaps on defense in the season-opening win against the Cleveland Browns. As the season wore on, Kendricks became more of a special teams player than a regular defensive one. He only played in 26.8 percent of the defensive snaps as opposed to 27.8 percent of the snaps.

Having to face teams such as the Washington Redskins, Dallas Cowboys, and New York Giants that utilize so many three WR sets called for more sub-packages. This meant one of the linebackers had to come off the field while a defensive back was inserted into the lineup.

Unfortunately for Kendricks, he was the linebacker that had to come out. The 2016 season was a humbling experience for Kendricks. He saw a drastic reduction in playing time and only started eight games.

After the season, Pederson endorsed Kendricks as a player that belonged in the scheme. "It's tough because he's that swing linebacker," Pederson said at his post-game press conference. "Teams play so much eleven personnel that, by the nature of the game, he's not on the field. Learning a new scheme, learning that position, I think he hung in there and battled."

"I think he's a perfect fit for this system, that backside linebacker because he can run sideline to sideline. He's a physical guy," Pederson continued. "Going into this off-season, he'll have a full year now, a full season of digesting the defense and the scheme, and expect some good things coming up through OTA's and next year in training camp."

Going from over 600 snaps in 2015 to 273 snaps in 2016 left a bad taste in Kendricks's mouth. He reportedly asked for a trade before the 2017 season. "It's cut and dry. That's the business. It's just like that. You tell them what you want. They either do it, or they don't, and you are in the contract that you signed. That's it," Kendricks said.

Keeping the Right Attitude

Kendricks had a $6.6 million cap hit in 2017. Rumors were circulating that Philadelphia would be interested in trading him to relieve themselves of the high cap hit for a player that wasn't considered a full-time starter.

Before the draft, the Eagles were reportedly close to trading Kendricks to the San Francisco 49ers. Those reports were weakened when San Francisco selected Alabama linebacker Reuben Foster at the bottom of the first round. Looking back on the situation, Kendricks acknowledged the sometimes short-term nature of the NFL. One team's trash can be another team's treasure.

"The trade door is never closed. There are a million teams out there," Kendricks said at his locker after practice early in training camp. "You only need one of them that loves you or likes what you are doing. Everyone is up. We are all renting space here, coaches included."

When it became clear that Kendricks would be with the Eagles in 2017, his focus was on being the best teammate he could be. Sure, he could have wondered what it would be like to be on a team that would give him more opportunities, but that was out of his control. "Those are all unknowns. I'm going to stay neutral on those types of questions because I am on this team, and I work next to these guys and have a duty on this team, and I respect these guys and the guys in the room that I work with every day," Kendricks said at the start of training camp in 2017. "Would I be better? Of course, we can sit here and say, 'Oh, I would be better here or there,' but that doesn't even matter because that's not the situation."

Kendricks said the Eagles told him he wouldn't be traded because he is 'young and talented' and they are not into trading away 'young and talented' players. Instead of feeling sorry for himself, Kendricks focused on what he was able to control which was how hard he worked. During training camp, Kendricks practiced with more energy. He started to show more flashes of the young, promising player that he was in 2014. There was a different fire that Kendricks played with, and it showed even in practice. He flowed to the football like he had a GPS tracker embedded in his uniform. Kendricks improved in his pass coverage. It showed when he took on running backs such as Darren Sproles, Donnel Pumphrey, and others during one on one pass coverage portions of practice.

Seeing Kendricks give post play guidance to younger players such as fellow linebacker Joe Walker wasn't a rarity. Kendricks seemed to be rejuvenated entering the 2017 season. Another sign that Kendricks was in a better place was his interaction with the media. Kendricks was more talkative in the locker room and more receptive to questions than he was in 2016.

Once the season started, Kendricks saw a slight uptick in playing time. He hovered around 37 percent of the defensive snaps in the first two games which came against the Washington Redskins and Kansas City Chiefs. Both teams forced the Eagles to be in more sub-packages which only use two linebackers on the field. Kendricks still managed to make the most of his playing time. He sacked Chiefs quarterback Alex Smith and had a pass breakup as well.

Despite thirsting for more playing time, Kendricks continued to press forward in 2017. That didn't go unnoticed by defensive coordinator Jim Schwartz. Schwartz praised Kendricks, but wouldn't reveal the details of any discussion they had about increased playing time.

"He's been a pro. I've said this from the beginning of training camp: He's gone out and worked really hard and done anything we've asked him to do," Schwartz said as the team prepared for a Week Four game against the Los Angeles Chargers. "Any conversations I have with the player I like to keep between the player and myself. I think from the very beginning of training camp, we talked about him coming into what he's going to be asked to do, and then doing that well. I couldn't be prouder of him."

Kendricks's pure talent as a player was on full display in Week Six against the Carolina Panthers on Thursday Night Football. He showed his coverage skills as he smothered Panthers running back Christian McCaffrey out of the backfield when he was assigned to do so. One of the plays caused Carolina quarterback Cam Newton to look for another pass catcher which resulted in a sack for the Eagles. Kendricks tracked Newton down as he tried to gain yards on the ground. Number 95 was all over the field in what was his best game with Schwartz as his defensive coordinator. He ended the game with 17 tackles, 12 of which were solo.

After the game, Kendricks was excited about getting a chance to make plays for his team.

"I think it's the opportunity. Last year was last year but this year is this year. I am getting a lot more opportunities," Kendricks said after the game. "When I get my opportunities, I take advantage of them. Stepping up to the plate when I got my opportunity was cool. A lot of things came my way, and it just worked out that way. Football is always fun, and we are winning right now. I am out here playing, so it's good. It's fun."

It was clear that Kendricks was finding his way in his second year playing in Schwartz's defense. The speed that Kendricks plays with was more evident because he was now able to just react to what he saw as opposed to taking time to process things.

"He's grown in the system, and he's gained more confidence, and he's gained more experience in the system. A lot is said of young players, rookies, the game slowing down," Schwartz explained during his weekly media availability. "Well, I think that applies to veteran players, whether it's a Patrick Robinson, a Corey Graham, guys that come in that are learning a new system. I'll bet you it's really fast for them in the beginning, a guy's first year in the program. But it's not his first year, it's his second year in the system, and he is a veteran player, and I think you're seeing the results of that."

It was good that Kendricks was settling in because middle linebacker Jordan Hicks ruptured his Achilles the following week against the Redskins and was placed on injured reserve. Hicks's injury paved the way for more playing time for Kendricks. But first, Kendricks had to work his way through a hamstring injury that limited him in practice that week and kept him out of the Redskins game.

Eagles coach Doug Pederson told the media he expected Kendricks to maximize his chance to play more with Hicks being done for the year. "It's a great opportunity for Mychal Kendricks," Pederson said before facing the 49ers in Week Eight. "And he's been a big part of the success on defense already this year, and I know his role's limited because of the style of offenses. You know, a lot of nickel and dime personnel on defense and obviously he was the guy coming out. But now this is a big opportunity for him. I fully expect him to rise to the occasion."

The following week Kendricks got the start and stayed on the field in nickel packages against San Francisco. He played a season-high 78.8

percent of the plays in the Eagles 33 – 10 thrashing of the 49ers. Kendricks finished with seven tackles, a sack, and a pass breakup.

"I think he's done a nice job with what we've asked him to do. I can go farther than covering running backs, but he's been a good blitzer, he's covered man-to-man well, and he's done a good job in our zone coverages," Schwartz said after the game. "He made a great play in the red zone knocking that ball down. That's a tough matchup. That guy is running an angle route, and Mych's athletic ability showed there. That was a big stop in that game."

Kendricks also drew praise from his position coach Ken Flajole. One thing that continues to come to the surface was how well Kendricks has handled the frustrating situation of not playing more and how he took advantage of more playing time when it presented itself. "He has done a great job. He's been very professional. When you are a competitive athlete, you want to be out there all of the time. I get that," Flajole said in a media session with assistant coaches during the bye week. "Unfortunately, with some of our packages, you can't have everybody out there. He has handled it great. Now that he's had the opportunity to play a little bit more with Jordan being down, he's done a nice job. He's been a joy to coach."

With Hicks gone, Kendricks didn't play less than 69 percent of the defensive snaps for the rest of the year with the exception of the regular season finale against the Dallas Cowboys. Only playing 22 percent of the snaps in that game was a sign that Kendricks had come full circle. The Cowboys game was a meaningless one to the Eagles. They already clinched the top seed in the NFC playoffs and had no reason to play the starters. Unlike those two preseason games in 2016, this time when Pederson rested the starters and key players, Kendricks was one of them.

Once the playoffs rolled around, Kendricks and the defense had the daunting task of slowing down the Atlanta Falcons high-powered offense in the divisional round. Having secured a first-round bye, the defense had a week to fine tune things before they knew who their opponent was going to be. The players along with coach Pederson decided to wear full pads during one of their practices to make sure they didn't lose track of the physicality that got them so far.

Once they found out the opponent was the Falcons, they went to work. Although the Eagles were the top seed, they were not favored to win the game against the Falcons. Their matchup came down to the wire with Philadelphia winning by a narrow margin. The 15 – 10 score was finalized on the last play of the game.

It went unnoticed for the most part, but Kendricks made a heads-up play that helped save the game.

Atlanta had the ball on the Eagles' two-yard line with 1:05 left in the game. Rather than run the ball against Philadelphia's stout defense, the Falcons elected to go with a pass play. All-Pro wideout Julio Jones lined up on the right side. The play called for quarterback Matt Ryan to sprint to the right and get the ball to Jones who was guarded by cornerback Jalen Mills. Running back Devonta Freeman threw a cut block on defensive end Vinny Curry on the opposite side which was where Kendricks was. As Ryan ran to the right side, Kendricks stayed home instead of chasing after him.

The decision to do his job, which was to cover the backside of the play, allowed Kendricks to see Freeman get up and release to the flat after diving at Curry's legs. Ryan knew that he had Freeman as an option on the backside of the route if Jones was covered. He looked back in Freeman's direction, but Kendricks had him covered. The old Kendricks that liked to freelance would have vacated his coverage assignment in hopes of tracking down the quarterback.

Now it was on to the Minnesota Vikings in the NFC Championship. This game was not only a clash of the top teams in the conference, but it was also a battle of the Kendricks brothers. Mychal's younger brother Eric was a selected by the Vikings in the second round (number 45 overall) of the 2015 NFL Draft. The two brothers were set to play on opposing teams for the right to go to the Super Bowl.

"It's unreal. . . . I mean, I've lived in a room with this kid for seventeen years, and we've pretty much lived the same lives," Mychal Kendricks said at his locker during the week leading up to the game. "Now we're on different teams, and we're in the same scenario, playing the same position. It's crazy man!"

Even though the game was in Philadelphia, the Vikings were favored to win. As it turned out, the bookies and analysts were wrong. The Eagles dominated Minnesota, winning the game by a score of 38 – 7 to set up a showdown with the New England Patriots in Super Bowl LII.

Mychal Kendricks had eight tackles in the win. Eric Kendricks had six tackles and two pass breakups. After the game, he expressed how frustrated he was to lose to his older brother. "I want to be there you know, I'm a competitor, and I play this game to win period. So I don't care if he's on the other team or not, I'm trying to win," the younger Kendricks brother said. "So right now I'm mad, yeah I'm not happy for him. It's crazy that we're in this position, all of the things that we've been through yeah that's cool. But, I'm not happy for him you know, I wanted to win that game. They beat us fair and square, and we'll see, but for right now, I'm not happy."

"I am a true believer in the universe and the cosmos working, the stars aligning. Things happen for a reason," Mychal Kendricks said after practice on Thursday. "It all worked out. I am standing here going to the Super Bowl, and I wouldn't want it any other way."

The Eagles had a week of practice in Philadelphia before parting for Minnesota for the week. After his final practice at the NovaCare Complex, Kendricks sat at his locker and reflected on the past couple of years. "I am having fun because I am playing. It's always fun to play the game. It's huge," Kendricks said with a big smile. "This is an opportunity for everyone. There's not one game on except for ours! That's hella tight! It's just on a larger scale, but it's a game nonetheless, so it's another opportunity to go out and show our talent."

"In the beginning, when I felt the way I felt, no one knew we'd be in this predicament," Kendricks said. "After this season, we are back at square one. Every season is a new season. You just have to make the most out of every opportunity. You may fall short due to a circumstance that you have no control over but you just have to keep a positive outlook on things and keep grinding then hopefully things will turn around."

The week leading up to Super Bowl LII exposed Kendricks and his teammates to a lot more media interaction than the regular season. Kendricks was asked everything from questions about Bitcoin to stock advice.

Having such a laid back personality allowed Kendricks to keep everything in perspective. "I try not to get, I mean there's a lot of ebbs and flows to this game, but I don't buy into it. Whatever is going to happen is going to happen. It's already written. My personality allows me to make calm out of the situation," Kendricks said three days before playing in Super Bowl LII. "We are in the Super Bowl, but I tell myself it's another game. There's a lot of hype involved. "It's the Super Bowl, so you're going to have 'super' everything. Super fans, super media, the whole thing is just super, but it's just another game for our team to get better and solidify who we are this season."

That laid-back personality was cast aside on game day. Kendricks was on the field for 80.6 percent of Philadelphia's defensive snaps. He finished with four tackles and two pass breakups. The Eagles beat the Patriots 41–

33 to bring the first Super Bowl win to Philadelphia. A few days later the city held one of the most epic championship parades ever.

As the Eagles paraded through Philadelphia on open-top tour buses, Kendricks walked on the side of his designated bus shaking hands with fans. Little did Kendricks know that would be the last time he got to interact with those fans as a member of the Eagles.

Kendricks was released at the start of voluntary OTAs the following May. He texted a message for NBC Sports Philly's John Clark to deliver to the fans the day his time in Philadelphia was brought to a close. "I love the Philly fans and I love Philly. We did something special this past year that no one can ever take away. I'll always cherish my time here in Philadelphia just off the simple fact that we won the first Super Bowl here together," Kendricks said. "Myself and the Philadelphia fans played a huge role in that. We truly won together and that's special. All good things have to come to an end and it's time for myself to start the next chapter of my career"

Player Spotlight: Jalen Mills

As the 2016 NFL Draft drew closer to its conclusion, former LSU defensive back Jalen Mills sat and waited for his name to be called. Finally, with the number 233 pick, Mills was selected by the Philadelphia Eagles.

It is hard to believe 232 prospects were better than Mills in 2016, but that's exactly how things shook out. Going from seventh-round pick to starter for a Super Bowl-winning team in one season is the kind of story that exemplifies bucking the odds. It had been a long journey for Mills from high school to college and ultimately to the NFL. If the journey wasn't so difficult, he would not have enjoyed the end result as much.

After sitting at his locker for the first time, Mills tried to grasp what he had accomplished by getting to the NFL. "Every time I come here and look at my locker, I just get chill bumps," Mills said.

Playing for one of the nation's best programs prepared Mills for the NFL. "Just going against the best players at practice. Then trying to convert now to the NFL, playing in the west of the SEC you are going against the best guys week in and week out," Mills said when he visited Tiger Stadium during the Eagles Week Four bye week. "You have to be mentally and physically prepared. Just transitioning over to the NFL wasn't easy but LSU prepared me a lot."

LSU head coach Les Miles was able to lure Mills to Baton Rouge after he was rated by Rivals.com as a three-star recruit. Mills transferred to DeSoto High School in Dallas for his senior season before heading to LSU.

Mills found instant success when he got to LSU. He started all 13 games at cornerback as a true freshman in 2012, recording 57 tackles and two interceptions. That year, he played in the same secondary as safety Eric Reid (49ers), and cornerback Jalen Collins (formerly of the Falcons). Mills stepped in for dismissed defensive back Tyrann Mathieu and played like a veteran from the start. Even though Mills never got to play in a game with Mathieu, the two kept in touch while Mills was at LSU.

Mathieu was thrown off the team in August 2012 due to violating team rules. Despite not playing in 2012, the Arizona Cardinals selected Mathieu in the third round (69th overall) of the 2013 NFL Draft.

"It was very big coming into my freshman year at LSU. Me going to LSU, he accepted me as his little brother," Mills said during his first press conference after rookie minicamp in 2016. "He has helped me in anything that I need on the field and off the field, just helping me be the best player that I can be."

Mills once again started all 13 games as a sophomore. He posted 67 tackles (third on the team), three sacks (tied for second), and three interceptions (tied with safety Craig Loston for team high). Adversity managed to find Mills before the start of his junior year. In June, Mills was arrested and facing a pending charge of second-degree battery by Baton Rouge Police.

The charges stemmed from an alleged occurrence with a woman that happened in May. Mills allegedly punched the woman in the mouth. Mills denied the allegations and his girlfriend admitted to assaulting the victim.

The original charges were dropped and reduced to a misdemeanor. Mills was ordered to complete a pre-trial diversion program in which he had to take drug tests, go under psychiatric evaluation, and pay $1,000 of the victim's medical bills.

LSU suspended Mills because of the infractions. Mills said he had a meeting with the dean as things started to come to light. Both he and the young woman gave statements. The dean got to decide whether or not Mills would be allowed back on campus again. She heard the statements and felt like his side was more of the truth.

Once he was able to put the issues aside, the versatility that Mills possesses started to show in his junior year. Mills started 13 games, all but one of them coming at safety. He also started at nickel corner in 2014. Although he only had one interception, Mills had five pass breakups to go along with 62 tackles, three of which were for a loss.

As a senior, Mills was poised to cap off a fairly productive career at LSU. Unfortunately, he missed the first five games of the season due to a leg injury he suffered during preseason practice. The injury happened in the final practice of the preseason when a teammate got pushed in the back and rolled up on Mills's ankle. He could have sat out the year and came back the following season. Rather than do that, Mills came back and played after he fractured his left fibula (leg) and tore ligaments in his ankle.

"I wanted to be back on the field with my teammates. I love the game. It is everything to me," Mills said. "I can't lie, the thought of red-shirting did kind of linger in my head, but once I was recovering so fast, I put it in my mind that I wanted to be back on the team and on the field with my teammates and my coaches."

Keith Allison

Jalen Mills

Mills played in the final six games of his senior year and posted 30 tackles, one sack, and three pass breakups. Senior Day was a special time for Mills because he got to face Texas A&M, which is where a lot of the Texas guys that he grew up with played their college ball.

The draft projections for Mills were all over the board. Some had him as high as a second-round prospect while others had him as low as a seventh rounder.

Mills spent the week at the Senior Bowl and showed that he was capable of playing safety or cornerback in the NFL. His versatility was something that many personnel people liked about him. How hard he competed was something else that stood out.

Mills was invited to the 2016 NFL Combine and ran a disappointing 4.61 second time in the 40-yard dash. He lowered the time to 4.48 seconds at LSU's Pro Day.

It was important for Mills to lower his 40 time because he wanted to emphasize his versatility as a defensive back. He needed to show that he was fast enough to turn and run with wide receivers if he was asked to play on an island.

"You've got guys who they say can play either position, and then you run slow," Mills told Nola.com after his Pro Day at LSU. "That's why I say for me, the big emphasis today was my forty, so guys wouldn't just say, 'Oh, well, he's just a safety' or 'he's just a nickel.' Now, it gets into that spot to where, 'Oh, yeah, he can play cornerback' and 'he can play the middle of the field and go hash to hash or sideline to sideline.'"

Mills's head coach endorsed him as a versatile defensive back that can also contribute on special teams. "He's very bright," LSU coach Les Miles said at Mills's Pro Day. "I think safety is certainly a place he can play. He can also play in coverage. You're looking at a guy who can line up in the slot, or in a season where you get a guy nicked he can step out and play corner in a heartbeat. Special teams, bright enough to make all the adjustments at safety. It's where we used him at the end of his career. We used him at corner at the beginning of his career. If an injury were to take place, he can step in and play significantly at the corner spot. Bright as a whip and talented. He ran 4.4 fast."

The scouts told Mills he looked phenomenal during his workouts. That still was not enough to get him selected towards the higher end of where his projections had him landing.

One of the reasons Mills fell was because of the questions surrounding his arrest in 2014, even though the charges were pending and eventually dropped. "From the Senior Bowl to the Combine that's something that I had to tell teams," Mills said. "Once I told them, all of the teams did their own private investigations, and the teams told me they felt like I was telling them the truth. They just wanted to hear that from me."

"The girl, it was her words against mine. She had witnesses, but I had several witnesses as well too. We carried on until the charges were dropped. The pre-trial program is something I decided to do because I didn't want to go to court and have it linger on. I plead 'no-contest' so I didn't get put on charges to where I was guilty of anything."

Having pending charges that involved striking a woman didn't convey the image that Mills wanted to portray of himself. It was something that bothered him for many reasons. "It's very hard. Through that whole situation, I grew up in a single-parent home with just my mom. She raised me," Mills explained, "My grandmother and my two aunts, me being raised around women taught me how to cater to a woman and how to love a woman, not to do those things that I was accused of. The hurt that I had wasn't for me because I knew I wasn't guilty. The hurt was for my mother and grandmother because they knew I wasn't raised like that and that I wouldn't do something like that."

The scouts were also reportedly down on Mills because of the injury that kept him from playing until later in the season even though he showed that it was clearly behind him.

There are certain intangibles that standout about a prospect that can only be sensed from watching him practice. While spending a week watching Mills at the Senior Bowl, the scouts for the Philadelphia Eagles got a chance to see how hard he competed. His passion for the game showed, especially during one on ones against the wideouts.

New head coach Doug Pederson wanted to add players that were passionate about the game and possessed an extreme thirst for competition. Witnessing Mills exhibit both traits made him an attractive prospect. Armed with eight picks in the 2016 NFL Draft, Executive VP of football operations Howie Roseman decided to use two of his draft picks on defensive backs. Roseman and the Eagles selected former Michigan and Auburn defensive back Blake Countess in the sixth round (number 196 overall). They followed up by selecting Mills with their next pick which came in the seventh round (number 233 overall). Dropping to the seventh round came as a surprise to Mills. It's something that added to an already existing chip on his shoulder.

"I have no idea why. The draft is crazy. I am just blessed to be in the position that I am and to be picked up by this team. I mean, it was very frustrating. I am pretty sure it was that way for a lot of other guys who weren't picked high. There's always a chip on my shoulder regardless of if I went first round or seventh. That's just the attitude that I play with on the football field. I always want to prove myself to the coaches and to my teammates. I want to be the best player on the field."

It didn't take long for Mills to win over the coaches and his new teammates. His willingness to compete was evident right away from rookie minicamp and carried over to when the veterans showed up for voluntary minicamp.

New defensive coordinator Jim Schwartz brought in some of the players he coached when he served in the same role with the Buffalo Bills in 2014. One of those players was cornerback Leodis McKelvin. McKelvin and returning veteran Nolan Carroll started out on top of the cornerback depth chart. Second-year defensive back Eric Rowe figured to be in the mix for a starting spot as well. However, Mills stood out more in minicamp and seemed to fit in better with the mindset that Schwartz was trying to establish on defense.

"He's been impressive so far. But we haven't really even started yet, to tell you the truth," Schwartz said during minicamp. "He's got a lot to learn, and his head's probably swimming a little bit. But what he has shown is he's a very good athlete. He can play the ball, and he's comfortable being on an island. I think if you were check-marking things for corners, those would be there near or at the top."

Mills started working with the first-team defense so the coaches could see him go against the starting wide receivers. He passed that test as he held his own against the likes of starting wideout Jordan Matthews and others.

"I love his competitiveness. I love the aggression that he has playing that position, and he doesn't back down from any of our veteran receivers or tight ends, or any of the guys that you normally might see on a normal basis might do that," Head coach Doug Pederson said when asked about Mills. "He's challenging guys. He's got great quickness and transition in and out of breaks; smart kid; eager to learn. Those are things that really have stood out with me."

The opportunity to go against the best wideouts on the team helped Mills get better. As they say, 'iron sharpens iron.' "Going against these receivers here and with the way these coaches have worked with me, I feel like I have gotten a hundred times better," Mills said after a minicamp practice. "These guys know their body. Take Jordan [Matthews], he is a big frame guy. He may give you a certain stem on a route and box you out."

Mills reported to training camp in July with his hair dyed green. Combined with his aggressive play on the field, Mills soon earned the nickname, 'Green Goblin.' The dog days of summer heat tested the players. That didn't keep Mills from shining at the start of training camp, but

Pederson looked forward to the opportunity to see the rookie cornerback in full pads. "He's doing a great job. He's a physical guy, he moves well, he's sharp. He's learning Coach Schwartz's system back there, and he's putting himself in a position to help us tremendously," Pederson said two days into training camp.

"I love the work these guys do in shorts and helmets, but sometimes, once you get the pads on, it becomes a different animal. Once we get into camp a week or so and the volume starts to increase just a little bit, we'll see exactly where these kids are. But right now I love where he's at. I love his attention to detail, his aggression, and he's making plays."

Eventually, Mills worked his way into the rotation with the starters. Schwartz had Mills working at left cornerback. One thing that became apparent was Mills' ability to pattern-match the wide receivers. There were times when it seemed like he knew exactly what route they were running against him. He learned to look across the formation with a broad scope which allowed him to pick up on certain things that receivers key in on before the snap. It helped him diagnose route combinations.

"The formation may tell me that I may get a double move on a play," Mills said. "The guy may look at the safety or linebacker just trying to see where the leverage is. I have learned to pay attention to the whole field and not be locked on one thing." As a result, Mills got his hands on a lot of passes. He caused numerous incompletions on his reps.

When the pads came on, Mills started to become more talkative in practice. It was almost like the contact made him come alive. Pads have a way of separating the men from the boys. It started to become clear that Mills was man enough to handle the intensity that comes with physical practices in pads. "He's showed up every day. He's had some ups and downs. But, you know, what I like about him is he's very competitive. He comes back, and he doesn't shy away from contact. He doesn't shy away from matchups. You need that in a corner. He's still young. He's still inconsistent. He's got his ups and his downs. But he comes ready to battle every day," Schwartz said of his young prospect.

There are times when Schwartz had his corners in man-coverage by themselves on the outside. Mills's ability to handle that task showed as he challenged the wideouts during practice. "If you're on the edge and you don't embrace being on that island, you're in the wrong business. You know you go around here, I mean, Philly's had a great history of some corners that were on islands that embraced that. I think Jalen has shown signs that he can do those things," Schwartz said.

Mills secured a spot on the team by the time the Eagles were ready to name their 53-man roster. More importantly, he was in the mix for significant playing time. Philadelphia was able to trade cornerback Eric Rowe to the New England Patriots on September 7 because of Mills's emergence. In return, the Eagles got an additional fourth-round pick in the 2018 NFL Draft.

Mills was an active player in the season opener against the Cleveland Browns. He played mostly on special teams but still got to see the field in select sub-packages. The second week of the season saw Mills get matched up with Chicago Bears wideout Alshon Jeffery.

NFL offensive coordinators pick up on tendencies. They saw how Mills likes to take chances and jump routes. He's an aggressive corner. Jeffery beat Mills early in the game for a 49-yard completion. The big play was a result of a double move that was put in to use Mills's aggressiveness against him. "The double move, I was too aggressive and trying to make a play out there. It was all eyes," Mills explained after the Bears game. "I need to be more patient. My eyes were on him, but I just tried to jump the route."

Mills has an uncanny way of not letting big plays get him down. Rarely is he seen carrying a bad play over to the next rep. That trait is a necessity for success at cornerback. "You have to make the next play. That's how it is every play, especially at my position. It has to be your mentality. We are playing against elite guys, and this is a passing league. Guys are going to catch the ball," Mills said.

"That's the name of the game. It has to be 'on to the next play.' For me, I am trying to eliminate that one play. If I can erase that one play, it's a different ballgame," Mills continued. "I am confident in myself. Having guys come to me after a play, guys like Rodney McLeod, Jenkins came to me—coach Schwartz—they were like, 'You know you can cover the route, and it was all on you. It was nothing he did. You were too aggressive.' Them showing me that they have confidence in me always puts confidence in me."

That confidence is what allowed Mills to bounce back and keep Jeffery bottled up for the rest of the game. The Eagles got an interception on one play in which Mills got his hands on Jeffery to slow him down at the line and knock off the timing of the route. Jeffery finished with 96 yards, most of which came on his one long reception. More importantly, Mills kept Jeffery out of the end zone.

Player Spotlight: Jalen Mills

Things didn't get any easier for Mills the following week. This time Mills was on the field for 88.3 percent of the defensive plays against the high-powered Pittsburgh Steelers offense in Week Three. Steelers receiver Antonio Brown is one of the NFL's most explosive and most difficult players to contain. As a rookie, Mills was matched up with Brown throughout the game.

Pittsburgh made it a point to get Brown his touches during the game. Brown finished with 12 receptions for 140 yards but did not find his way to the end zone.

The All-Pro had a solid game statistically, but Mills made a good impression on Brown.

"He told me that he respected me and loved the fact that I was battling with him on every play, regardless of what was happening," Mills said. "I told him, 'Thank you.' Just being a late-round draft pick to becoming the player that he is right now. I thanked him for showing me what I need to work on."

Once nickel cornerback Ron Brooks ruptured his quadriceps tendon in Week Seven against the Minnesota Vikings, Mills was a more regular part of the rotation. Mills's next big test was taking on another one of the best wideouts in New York Giants' receiver Odell Beckham Jr. It was a renewal of an old rivalry they had from their days together at LSU. "Odell is a friend, and he was a teammate, but once that clock starts, it's the Philadelphia Eagles vs. the New York Giants. I know him well, I went to college with him for two years. I am not sure if I will be isolated against him and I honestly don't care," Mills explained during the days leading up to their Week Eight clash.

"You just try to stay focused on the game plan as well as the techniques that I have been trained to use. You want to bring physicality every week. You watch on certain plays to not be over-physical or try to do too much. That is when mishaps happen and big plays."

The Giants beat the Eagles 28-23 even though Beckham only had four receptions for 46 yards. But two of those four receptions were for touchdowns. Mills didn't play much, so he wasn't matched up against Beckham in their first meeting. That would change when they met again later in the season.

In the second to last game of the year, Mills was the primary defender charged with covering Beckham after he torched the Eagles for most of the game. Desperately clinging to a five-point lead, Philadelphia was in need of a defensive stop. Veteran safety Malcolm Jenkins suggested using Mills in man coverage against Beckham but also have box-and-one coverage around him by adding safety Terrence Brooks to the lineup. The plan kept Beckham from having a catch on the last drive by New York and resulted in an interception by Brooks to seal the 24 – 19 win for the Eagles.

Beckham had plenty of praise for his former college teammate after the game. "He has always been a confident person. It's one thing to just be confident, but it's another thing to be confident and back it up. That's what he does," Beckham said.

Philadelphia's coaching staff asked Mills to take on some of the game's best receivers, and he never backed down or wavered. There were times when he got beat, but Mills always bounced back. The confidence that he played with as a rookie made Schwartz really take to Mills in their first year together.

"I love the hell out of that kid. I really do," the defensive coordinator said at his press conference on Tuesday after the Giants game. "He is a competitor. People talk about speed, people talk about the ability to play the ball. To me, the number one criteria for playing corner is you have to be a competitor, and he is."

With his rookie year in the books, Mills set his sights on a more prominent role on defense the following season. It was pretty much a given that he would be a starting cornerback in 2017. The Eagles were very thin at cornerback after electing not to re-sign Leodis McKelvin and Nolan Carroll. It was a foregone conclusion that they would select one in the 2017 NFL Draft.

With Mills set as one of the starters, the Eagles signed free agent Patrick Robinson to compete for a starting spot opposite Mills. They also selected cornerbacks Sidney Jones (number 43 overall) and Rasul Douglas (number 99 overall) in the draft. Jones had ruptured his Achilles tendon during his Pro Day at Washington and was likely out for the year, but Douglas was able to compete immediately.

Jenkins projected Mills to step up in his second season and become a mainstay in the starting lineup. Having seen Mills hold his own against the top receivers in 2016, Jenkins was confident that he would elevate his game the following year. "We have a lot of faith in Jalen Mills," Jenkins said in the spring of 2017. "I am excited to watch him mature into a starting cornerback, and I think he is going to have a breakout season. We are going to put a lot of pressure on Mills to step up and be that guy for us."

"I am impressed by his mentality and approach to the game. At the corner position, that is ninety percent of what it is," Jenkins continued. "He also has the athletic gifts. His competitiveness and willingness to work to get better day-in and day-out has been impressive since he got here and hasn't changed. As we push a little more load onto him, he can handle it."

Mills went through OTAs and minicamp as the starting left cornerback. Like he did as a rookie, Mills got his hands on the football consistently. His confidence and swagger showed as he started to emerge as a leader in the secondary. Mills also began to use the finger wave gesture after a pass directed his way fell incomplete.

The competition increased in practice after the Eagles signed free agent wide receivers Torrey Smith and Alshon Jeffery. A much improved Nelson Agholor also gave Mills a challenge in practice. Mills played well in training camp, but Robinson, a new addition to the secondary struggled. Philadelphia knew it was time to make a move, so they traded Jordan Matthews and a third-round pick to the Buffalo Bills in exchange for cornerback Ronald Darby.

Darby was inserted on the starting defense at right corner opposite of Mills. The move gave the Eagles two aggressive cornerbacks on the outside that liked to jump routes and provided sticky coverage against receivers.

Schwartz pointed to Mills as one of the most improved players on defense. He really liked how Mills seemed to settle in on the outside and adopt a role as a leader. Oftentimes it was Mills who delivered some parting words and broke down the secondary in their group huddle after practice. It came naturally to him even though he was a younger player. He'd do the same thing before the defensive backs ran out on the field for pregame warmups.

Mills notched his first career interception against the Washington Redskins in the season opener. He picked off an errant pass by quarterback Kirk Cousins in the end zone which stopped what seemed like a scoring drive for the Redskins.

Two games later, Mills was once again faced with covering Beckham and the Giants. Beckham beat Mills for two touchdowns that day, but the Eagles came out on top. Even though Mills gave up both scores, he still drew praise from Schwartz after the game. "I was proud of Jalen. He did a very good job of limiting big plays. He gave up two touchdowns, but they were short passes. He was targeted twenty-something times. He never once came to the sideline asking for help, and the biggest part of it is he shadowed one of the best receivers in the NFL," Schwartz said.

"When we needed a big stop, he came down with that play. The short memory is a good thing for a corner. I love his competitiveness. That took every bit of his competitiveness to be able to survive that game."

Mills said the coaches came to him the Thursday before the game to tell him that Beckham was going to be his assignment. After the game Mills was disappointed in the touchdowns that he gave up but was glad the coaching staff trusted him to shadow Beckham. "It means that they trust me. But at the same time, that also goes with the practice, playing hard, practicing hard, and showing effort all of the time," Mills said after the game.

Mills had 12 tackles and two pass breakups against the Giants. It's safe to say he was very busy that week. Offenses tried to attack Mills early in the season. After the 20 targets he faced against the Giants, Mills hovered around 42 passes that were thrown his way through the first three weeks. He was one of the most targeted corners in the league.

Mills and the defense hit a groove over a stretch of the season, establishing themselves as one of the top units in the NFL. After intercepting a pass by C. J. Beathard and returning it 37-yards for a touchdown, Mills was named the NFC Defensive Player of the Week in Week Eight.

Having returned six interceptions for touchdowns over his career, Malcolm Jenkins knows a thing or two about return skills. Jenkins and the Eagles secondary coaches had been joking with Mills for not cashing in on opportunities to reach the end zone.

"I've been getting on him for not having a lot of returns. That was a good one," Jenkins said. "He shut me up on that play. We've been doing a decent job of getting turnovers, but scoring on those opportunities is something we wanted to take the next step to. Every day I'm messing with him about his lack of return skills. That was a pretty good return."

Mills broke down how he was able to make the big play when he looked back on it after practice the following Wednesday. "Once I seen the tight end motion over, I knew I was going to be one-on-one with Garcon. Just knowing that he was the best route runner and receiver on the team, they were eventually going to try and get something going. I knew I had to lock in and once I seen him give me a slight stem and straighten back up, just watching film, I knew that route was coming. I trusted myself and trusted my safety to be over the top and break on the ball.

"It's film study, one hundred percent, that's all it is—film study. It's like going into a test and it's true or false and you're like, 'I don't know.' But if you know it, you're going to attack the answer. I was about to go out of bounds, but then I thought about it. Malcolm [Jenkins], Coach Schwartz [defensive coordinator Jim Schwartz], and Coach Undlin [defensive backs coach Cory Undlin] . . . have been grilling me all week, talking about I had no return skills. I had to cut it back and get in the end zone or I wouldn't have stopped hearing that, for sure."

After seeing how Mills jumped the route to garner an interception, offenses once again started to target Mills with double moves. Mills gave up two touchdowns on slant and go routes in back-to-back games against the Giants and Oakland Raiders.

New York receiver Tavarres King beat Mills in the red zone, getting him to bite on the slant before turning upfield and hauling in a 13-yard touchdown catch on a pass from Eli Manning. The following week, Amari Cooper got Mills to do the same thing as he and Raiders quarterback David Carr connected on a 63-yard touchdown. Mills vowed to stay aggressive. That is what allowed him to break up 21 passes in his first two seasons.

Philadelphia was still able to beat the Giants and Raiders, allowing them to secure the home-field advantage throughout the playoffs. Their first playoff game came against the Atlanta Falcons. That game went down to the wire. The Falcons had the ball at the two-yard line with just over a minute left in the game, threatening to take the lead. All-Pro wideout Julio Jones had his way with the Eagles' defense up to that point. He had 101 yards on nine receptions.

Atlanta broke the huddle and Jones trotted to Mills's side. Moving on to the next round or going home came down to the result of the play. It was clear that Jones was going to get the ball. He released off the line of scrimmage and tried to initiate contact with Mills before pushing off and fading to the corner of the end zone. Mills used excellent technique as he wisely cut off Jones's path, escorting him towards the sideline. By doing that, Mills pinched the cushion for quarterback Matt Ryan to drop the ball into Jones's hands.

Ryan attempted to get the ball to Jones anyway, but it fell incomplete as Jones and Mills went up for the contested throw. The game was over, and the Eagles had a 15-10 victory allowing them to advance to the NFC Championship game.

After watching from the sideline, tight end, Zach Ertz gave his take on Mills's defensive stop. "I thought Jalen [Mills] had amazing coverage," Ertz said after the game. "I kind of saw that play coming when he got to the back of the end zone, and it was sprint-out; that's kind of his staple—the sprint-out play. And Jalen did an amazing job."

Next up for the Eagles was the NFC Championship game. The Minnesota Vikings were no match for the Eagles at Lincoln Financial Field in the NFC Championship game. Mills and the defense held the Vikings offense to one touchdown in a 33-7 win and advanced to Super Bowl LII. As one of the starters on defense, Mills got the chance to have his own podium during a couple of the media availability sessions during Super Bowl week in Minnesota. The once seventh-round pick had come a long way since he entered the NFL in 2016. He had become very close with his fellow defensive backs.

Now he was on the biggest stage the league has to offer. Mills opened up about the brotherhood the defensive backs have and how it allowed them to trust each other so much on the field. "It starts at the DB dinners that we do once a week. Trusting guys and getting more comfortable with guys so when you get out there on the field, there are no issues," Mills explained. "Once we get in the meeting room, we are talking it out. Nobody is stuck in their ways. Nobody sees themselves bigger than the next man. When you have that type of unity, you have big-time trust out there on the field."

That trust was tested to the fullest against Tom Brady and the New England Patriots in Super Bowl LII. Brady finished with 505 yards passing, and three touchdown passes. Mills had nine tackles and two pass breakups in the Eagles 41 – 33 win. He was one of several defenders in position to keep All-Pro tight end Rob Gronkowski from coming down with a jump ball as seconds ticked off the clock.

After reaching the ultimate goal in football, Mills shared an event from his past that helped him learn about dealing with adversity. "One of the biggest things from my career was when I broke my leg my senior year at LSU. I remember sitting in my house with one of my friends and just telling him that it might be over for me," Mills said in May when voluntary OTAs started. "Then having to reevaluate myself and my life to fight through that adversity. Having to work back to this and getting to win Super Bowl LII."

The win was the first Super Bowl victory in franchise history. Philadelphia celebrated the win by throwing a parade for the Eagles. The parade was the icing on the cake for Mills. "It still goes back to the adversity part of the season happening. Then going to the parade and seeing all of those people and how much love they were showing us and how happy the team was and the coaching staff was. Everybody that was around us, you felt the love," Mills explained. "All I was thinking about was [we] were just talked about so badly. Regardless of how our record looked, we were talked about like we were trash, but look at how beautiful the parade was. It was like a rose growing from the concrete. Everybody had us paved in concrete and you see the parade it was just like a rose, a beautiful flower."

Player Spotlight: Nelson Agholor

One of the best stories for the 2017 Philadelphia Eagles was the emergence of wide receiver Nelson Agholor. He turned the tide in his favor and became one of the team's deadliest offensive players.

It had been a long road for Agholor, but he began to scratch the surface of his potential as a playmaker in 2017. However, it wasn't always such a promising outlook. As his teammates suited up and prepared to run out of the tunnel at Lincoln Field for pregame intros, Eagles wide receiver Nelson Agholor donned a green team-issued parka and black winter hat. Philadelphia was getting ready for their game against the Green Bay Packers in Week Twelve during the 2016 season.

Agholor was deactivated for the game after a tough outing the previous week against the Seattle Seahawks. He had a drop on a deep crossing route that would have led to a big gain. Agholor was also called for an illegal formation penalty that negated a long catch and run by tight end Zach Ertz that would have resulted in a touchdown.

After the game, then-wide receivers coach Greg Lewis was at Agholor's locker talking to the young wideout, who was clearly bothered by his performance. He opened up during a media scrum at his locker after the game. "I hate not competing at the level that I know I as an individual can compete at. It's about mentally being in my own head and taking away from the energy that I need to give to my teammates. Mentally, I can put myself in a storm, but I need to jump out of the storm," Agholor explained. "I just have to get out of my own head. I'm pressing so much and worried about so many things. I'm thinking too much and it's a selfish thing that needs to stop. I started getting in my own head and trying so hard to think about being perfect. Miscues were there, and I let it just eat at me."

The emotional press conference was a buildup of things that happened during his first two seasons in the NFL. Fans and media types wrongly labeled him a bust instead of giving him a chance to find his way in the league.

Agholor wasn't used to that kind of treatment because up to his time in the NFL, he had always exhibited excellence on the football field. However, he was prepared to weather the storm, but it was going to take time.

As a young boy, Agholor was raised in a strict household. His father, Felix Agholor is a former professional soccer player. "At the end of the day, you were prepared to deal with the ups and downs. You have to deal with making sure you lived the right way and did the right things consistently," Agholor said about his upbringing.

He described his father, a strict disciplinarian, as the 'total package,' while his mother was considered to be a great communicator. Those communication skills were utilized when Agholor's mother explained why his father disciplined them. That helped him understand the 'why' behind the discipline he received. Agholor refers to the authority in the household that he grew up in as a partnership between his mother and father.

The no-nonsense approach that was instilled in Agholor at home traveled to high school with him when he started playing for Berkeley Prep High School in Tampa, Florida. Agholor committed to getting better by doing extra sprints and watching a lot of film. It was a daily grind that just went from week to week with the reward being the results on game day then it was back to work.

"Victories were short-lived because Saturday was another day of conditioning and Sunday was a day to get more film to get ready for Monday's practice," Agholor said. "It was just like living a life on a regimen so even if things shook up and didn't go perfectly, you were so prepared that you just focused on playing."

There seemed to be a perfect synergy between Agholor's parents and his head coach Dominick Ciao when it came to the daily approach to life. Agholor's parents encouraged him to focus on every day and not only control that day, but maximize it.

"The advice from me was to always go a day at a time. Even a play at a time. That's the approach that he has," Ciao said in a phone interview. "The success that he has now is great but he has to keep on working and stay humble. The old saying by John Wooten is, 'Make each day your masterpiece.' That's what he tries to do."

Each day was a masterpiece for Agholor and it yielded plenty of results in the long-term. Agholor was rated by Rivals.com as a five-star recruit and was ranked as the third-best wide receiver in his class. Despite being recruited by two of the major schools in his home state, Agholor committed to USC in January 2012 over Alabama, Notre Dame, Oklahoma, Florida, and Florida State.

Alabama's wide receiver coach at the time was a guy by the name of Mike Groh. Groh later became Agholor's receiver coach with the Eagles and had a large part in his breakout season in 2017. Agholor hit the ground running at USC, playing in all 13 games as a true freshman posting 19 receptions for 340 yards and two touchdowns. The following year, Agholor was named a starter and his performance expanded to a return role as well.

He continued to excel as a sophomore. Besides catching 56 passes for 918 yards and six touchdowns, Agholor returned 18 punts for 343 yards and two touchdowns, and 10 kickoffs for 175 yards. Agholor was recognized as a second-team All-American by multiple sports outlets for his punt returning.

In his first two seasons at USC, Agholor had Jacksonville Jaguars wide receiver Marqise Lee on the opposite side of him. Lee won the 2012 Fred Biletnikoff Award as the top wide receiver in the nation after putting up 118 catches for 1,721 yards and 14 touchdowns.

Lee and Agholor were very similar wideouts in terms of body type and route running ability. Agholor also spent one season with Rams wide receiver Robert Woods at USC. After a dropoff statistically in 2013 (57 rec, 791 yds, four TDs), Lee declared for the 2014 NFL Draft. Agholor was now the top dog in the receiver group.

Looking back on his first two years at USC, Agholor felt it worked in his favor to have guys to learn from when he got there. "I wanted to learn how to play the position. It actually helped that they had two receivers there before me," Agholor said at the NFL Combine in 2015.

The 2014 season is when he cemented himself as one of the best players in the country. Agholor proceeded to explode for 104 receptions for 1,313 yards and 12 touchdowns as a junior. He elected to forego his senior year and enter the 2015 NFL Draft.

While at the NFL Combine in 2015, Agholor was asked what made him different from some of the other receiver prospects. His answer traced back to his high school days as a running back. "It actually helped that I played running back before there. It took my game to another level. I had more of an aggressive mentality when I caught the ball," Agholor said. "The end result was more yards after contact. As a running back, you are thinking big play every time. To have that mentality as a receiver, when you catch the ball you are thinking to get vertical, not first downs. When contact comes, you're not falling down. You run through contact and keep going."

Agholor's athleticism was on full display during the on-field workouts at the Combine. He caught the ball consistently and showed that he has the necessary straight-line quickness (4.43 seconds in 40-yard dash) to go along with the quickness that led to many big plays at USC.

Agholor had an informal meeting with the Eagles at the Combine in Indianapolis. In head coach Chip Kelly's final season at Oregon, he saw Agholor's explosiveness first-hand during his freshman season at USC. Kelly's Ducks beat USC in a 62 – 51 shootout, but Agholor had six receptions for 162 yards and a touchdown. One of Agholor's catches resulted in a 76-yard touchdown.

Some draft analysts compared Agholor to then-Eagles wide receiver Jeremy Maclin because of their similar size and ability to impact the game as returners as well as wideouts. Maclin had a monstrous year in Philadelphia before signing with the Kansas City Chiefs as a free agent. Kelly had to replace the 85 receptions for 1,318 yards and 10 touchdowns that was lost when Maclin left. The Eagles selected Agholor with the 20th overall pick in the 2015 NFL Draft to be their next playmaker.

"He's a great fit for what we're doing. He has excellent speed, outstanding hands, he's an outstanding route runner, and he's a student of the game," Kelly said after selecting Agholor. He's a real versatile guy, he can line up anywhere. He's dialed in as a football player, always striving to be better. He has a growth mindset, not a fixed mindset."

While at USC, Agholor worked in a pro-style system that allowed him to gain experience running most of the routes he would be asked to run in the NFL. As a junior, he played in more of an up-tempo offense that still had pro concepts. The faster pace on offense was similar to what Kelly used in Philadelphia. Naturally, it was assumed that Agholor would be a fit with the Eagles right away. Agholor liked the chances for him to make a smooth transition because of the familiarity.

"It's a wonderful opportunity for me. I came from a college system where we did similar things. I feel I have a great opportunity to continue to grow daily," Agholor said after the Draft

Kelly had a good relationship with Agholor's college coach Lane Kiffin, so his understanding of the things Agholor did at USC was extensive. He got to talk with Kiffin and Agholor's second college coach Steve Sarkisian about Agholor before the Draft and came away impressed.

Actually meeting with Agholor had Kelly and the Eagles even more impressed with the young prospect. "He's like a sponge when it's just the game of football. When he came here, and we had him on a visit here, we were in the room with him for a long time because of the questions he had for us about, 'How do we attack this coverage, and what do we do here?' He's one of those guys that's really a student of the game," Kelly said at a post-draft press conference. "I think you get excited when you're around guys like that. He's just trying to soak up everything that you can spit out in terms of being able to give him coaching points.

"He's always trying to get better, whether it's from a physical standpoint, improving himself physically, or a route-running standpoint, or just a mind standpoint regarding how to run routes, how to do things, and how does he fit into the scheme."

Agholor got off to a good start in training camp. He showed the playmaking ability that made him one of the best wideouts in the rookie class. "When Nelson gets the ball in his hands, he's real explosive, so you're anticipating run after the catch with him," Kelly said. "He did that a ton in college. He was also a great returner, so he's a dynamic player. That's why we drafted him so high."

That explosiveness showed in Agholor's first preseason game. He caught a high pass from Mark Sanchez against the Indianapolis Colts and took it to the end zone for a 34-yard touchdown. Agholor ended the day with three receptions for 57 yards and a touchdown.

Agholor earned a starting spot at wide receiver over veteran wideout Miles Austin and second-year receiver Josh Huff. When the 2015 regular season started, Agholor was a starter along with Jordan Matthews and Riley Cooper.

After starting the season with only one reception for five yards against the Atlanta Falcons, Agholor had three receptions for 31 yards against the Dallas Cowboys in Week Two. Agholor had the best statistical game of his rookie year against the Washington Redskins in Week Four. He caught three passes for 64 yards including a 45-yard reception in which he beat cornerback Chris Culliver and snagged the ball with one hand.

A high ankle sprain suffered the next game, which was against the New Orleans Saints, prevented Agholor from being able to build off the momentum from the Redskins game. The high ankle sprain kept Agholor out until Week Ten. The injury robbed Agholor of the quickness that he usually played with. Except for a Week Fourteen game against the Buffalo Bills in which he scored a 53-yard touchdown, Agholor was relatively quiet for the rest of his rookie season.

"A high ankle sprain is no joke, especially for a guy like Nelson. He's bouncy man," Jordan Matthews said during minicamp in 2016 when asked about Agholor's injury. "You can tell how he runs routes: it's tap, tap, tap. When you take that away from him—that is one of his strengths. It can do something to you not only physically but mentally also."

Agholor finished his rookie year with a disappointing 23 receptions for 283 yards and a touchdown. The instant success of rookie receivers from the 2014 NFL Draft class such as Odell Beckham Jr., Brandin Cooks, Kelvin Benjamin, and Eagles teammate Jordan Matthews set high expectations for any rookie class going forward.

The fact that fellow first-round pick Amari Cooper had 72 receptions for 1,070 yards and six touchdowns didn't help matters either. A lot of impatient fans called Agholor a bust after one season in the NFL. They expected instant success from Agholor.

"Naturally that stigma that a person is a first round pick, you're not a person anymore," Matthews said. "Now he's compared to every other first round pick and doesn't have the ability to just go out and work at the level and growth level that Nelson Agholor was meant to grow."

Head coach Chip Kelly was fired before the 2015 season ended. Doug Pederson was brought in from Kansas City to replace him after serving as the Chiefs offensive coordinator. Pederson brought his West Coast offense with him which focused on getting the ball into the playmaker's hands and allowing them to get yards after the catch. This kind of scheme was tailor-made for a player with Agholor's skill set.

Former Eagles wide receiver Greg Lewis was brought in to coach the receivers. Lewis was excited to work with Agholor and predicted a big season from the talented player. "Honestly, I wanted to get Agholor down in New Orleans when I was down there last year [working as an offensive assistant]," Lewis said in February 2016. "He was the best interview, the smartest, . . . and then you turn on his tape, and it's remarkable. Last year, he had some injuries that he dealt with, and it slowed him down some, but the athletic ability, the tools are all there for him to take. I think he's going to have a big jump from last year."

Pederson named Matthews and Agholor as the starting receivers on the outside. Agholor recognized how he had a golden opportunity in 2016. "Looking at last season, I did not take advantage of a good opportunity," Agholor said. "That is what I want to do this year, take advantage of a great opportunity. My route-running allows me to be the island guy, the 'X' receiver that goes against man coverage. I can tell you this year, the offense has done a great job of getting guys in position to execute against different coverages."

Agholor found himself in a little bit of trouble soon after his first mandatory minicamp under Pederson. The second-year receiver was accused of sexual assault stemming from an incident at a Gentleman's Club in Philadelphia. Reports began to surface that Agholor was set up by one of the employees at the club. Agholor hired Fortunato "Fred" Perri Jr., a prominent defense attorney in Philadelphia. Just over a month later, then Philadelphia District Attorney Seth Williams released a statement saying there was not enough evidence to file charges. Agholor was able to now focus on rebounding from a tough rookie season.

"I fell short in my mission," Agholor said when asked about representing the organization off the field. "I understand I should've done a better job. From here on out I have an obligation to do the right thing, to be the right person for this organization. I had to realize that I put myself in this position. Just continue to grow and also train. I couldn't let this defeat me twice. What would've happened to me if I would've just sat around moping? I wouldn't have been prepared to perform today. So I just continued to train, stay with my family, and get myself ready."

Pederson was ready to move on as well. He welcomed Agholor back for training camp.

"I just know this, that everybody, we all make mistakes, we learn from them, we move on, and we just look forward to him getting to camp and getting ready to go," Pederson said when the rookies reported.

Agholor worked through training camp and impressed the coaching staff with quickness off the line and within his routes. He worked to get better and catch the ball more consistently during practice, staying afterward to catch the ball off the jugs machine.

The only preseason game in which Agholor had a catch was against the Pittsburgh Steelers in the second week of the preseason. He had two receptions for 30 yards but also had a dropped pass to his credit. The drops were something that plagued the Eagles receiver group in 2015. They hoped to minimize them in 2016. Agholor had a few drops that made people question whether or not he was worthy of being a first-round pick.

His teammate Jordan Matthews came to Agholor's defense and praised him for the effort he puts forth on the field. Matthews preached patience with Agholor. "It gets lost in the shuffle because of trends," Matthews said.

"Jordy Nelson is one of my favorite receivers, I love him. He didn't get 1,000 yards until year four. Put it in perspective, guys get better. I look for attitude and effort. Does Nelson bring attitude and effort? Yes!"

Pederson said he felt Agholor was on the right track and that he wasn't concerned about Agholor after he had a drop against the Indianapolis Colts in the third preseason game. The coach pointed to the effort that Agholor gave as a blocker as a way to praise him.

The Eagles won the season opener against the Cleveland Browns. It was coach Pederson's debut, and Agholor hooked up with rookie quarterback Carson Wentz for a 35-yard touchdown in the game. Agholor was relatively quiet for most of the 2016 season. The dropped passes continued to happen as the team struggled through a streak in which they only won once in four games. After a loss against the Dallas Cowboys in overtime, Agholor was asked about the dropped passes by some of the pass-catchers up to that point.

At the end of the day, man, that [expletive] means nothing. You just got to make the next one. Everybody runs routes. Sometimes they're contested. Sometimes we drop them, but if you make as many as you possibly can that come your way, you're going to put yourself in a good position.

No one's perfect. I don't look at no drops, that type of [expletive]. I'm tired of hearing it. It's stupid. We play football. I dropped the first one. I ain't dropped one after that.

What does it matter? Because if we lose now we're going to place blame on this person did this. No, as a team we got a responsibility to win football games, and I get it, some plays could have helped. But there's still four quarters of football to be played.

The specific play that Agholor was personally under fire for was a slant that he dropped in the first quarter that would have resulted in a first down instead of forcing the Eagles to punt. To Agholor's credit, he made a couple of catches in traffic against the Cowboys later in the game.

Coach Pederson had been working to establish a specific culture in Philadelphia during his first year. He wanted to build a family type atmosphere. When a true family exists, they are not afraid to hold each other accountable and offer correction when need be. That's exactly what Pederson did regarding Agholor's comments after the Cowboys game. "I'm disappointed in the type of comments. I think each individual has to be responsible for their own job, obviously," Pederson said the Monday after the game. "We got to make good, smart choices. Everybody is mad and disappointed and angry after tough losses like we just came through. Cooler heads prevail, and we just have to bite our lip sometimes, and suck it up and get to work."

There were flashes, but the dynamic playmaker that dominated the PAC-12 conference as a junior at USC didn't show up every week like he did in college. Agholor's comments after the Cowboys game was a sign that the pressure was starting to get to him. He was pressing too much instead of allowing the game to come to him.

That leads us back to the Seahawks game in Week Eleven. That was a bottoming out period for Agholor. One play exemplified the good and the bad of Agholor. Agholor lined up against All-Pro cornerback Richard Sherman in the series after his penalty negated a Zach Ertz touchdown. He stemmed his route inside perfectly and gave Sherman a subtle move at the top of the route like as if he was going to drive to the outside.

Sherman bit on the move and Agholor separated from him as he flattened his routes across the middle of the field. Quarterback Carson Wentz saw Agholor come open and delivered a strike to him. Agholor failed to focus on the ball and had his hands positioned incorrectly, allowing it to get to his body and fall incomplete.

Wentz stood up for Agholor when asked about remaining confident in him after the dropped pass. "When that happens, it's tough, but you move on," Wentz said after the game. "Obviously, it's frustrating, but I am coming back to him the next play. We have not lost confidence in him! I have not lost confidence in him. We just have to keep encouraging him."

'Go back to him' is precisely what Wentz did when he looked to Agholor on a two-point conversion later in the game. Agholor caught the ball cleanly as he crossed the goal line. Wentz credited Agholor for 'working his tail off.' He pointed out how no one sees the things he does to get better after practice.

While fans were mad at Agholor for eliminating Ertz's touchdown, the tight end refused to criticize his struggling teammate. "I'm not mad at him at all," Ertz said after the game. "It's not my job to critique how he plays. He's trying his best, that's all you can really ask. I don't think he went out before the play and said, 'I'm going to take a touchdown away.' We made a lot of mistakes, dropping the ball, false start penalties, holding penalties, pick penalties."

Pederson vowed to keep encouraging Agholor as he went through the troubled times. He said Agholor has met with an Eagles team psychologist to discuss some of the issues at hand. "Any time a player goes through a rough spell, it can play on the psyche of the player," Pederson explained. "From my standpoint as a coach, I have to tell him to keep fighting. He has to fight through it. He has to learn to not listen to the outside world."

Once a natural receiver, Agholor was at times fighting the football as he tried to catch it. It seemed like he was telling himself that he cannot drop the pass rather than just make the catch. Pederson elected to deactivate Agholor for the Packers game the following week so he could take a step back and try to clear his mind. It seemed to work. For the first time, Agholor started to say his focus was on having fun playing football. That new approach was good for him because it encouraged him to relax and appreciate the athletic gift he was given. Agholor took a step back and thought about why he was struggling. He thought about how the pressure was getting to him and being too concerned about what the outside voices thought of him. The only thing that should have mattered was what his coaches and teammates thought of him.

"I told him he can't think about it. I don't know what he reads," teammate Jordan Matthews said. "I told him not to read any of that stuff. It's not healthy. The worst thing you can do is bring other stuff outside of your job to your job."

Agholor realized he was playing a game that he enjoyed and wanted to get back to that as opposed to focusing on the pressure to perform. "I am going to make sure I am putting an emphasis on having fun," Agholor said. "When you have fun, you don't even think, you react. God gave me great abilities, and now I am in a position where I need to take advantage of it. I am excited to get back after it."

Agholor was back on the field for the next game, which was a 32 – 14 beatdown at the hands of the Cincinnati Bengals. He resumed his role as a starter and played in each of the final games down the stretch. Other than a 40-yard touchdown reception against the New York Giants in Week Sixteen, Agholor didn't do much statistically. Being able to close the book on the 2016 season was a good thing for Agholor and the Eagles. They had something big in store for the following year.

Wide receivers coach Greg Lewis was let go during the offseason. After being fired by Pederson, Lewis went to Kansas City to coach the Chiefs' receivers. After a brief search, Pederson hired Mike Groh to take over as receivers coach. Groh had recruited Agholor out of high school back when he coached the receivers at Alabama. A lot of receivers that worked with Groh in the past had their best seasons under him. Things were looking up for Agholor.

Former Chicago Bears receiver Alshon Jeffery was one of the receivers that found success under Groh. With Groh as his coach, Jeffery had his best season in 2013. He posted 89 receptions for 1,421 yards and seven touchdowns. The Eagles signed Jeffery to a one-year contract after making another move to bring in former Baltimore Ravens and San Francisco 49ers wideout Torrey Smith.

Agholor had already known Jeffery through a mutual trainer in Tampa. Having Jeffery in the fold helped Agholor—who refers to Jeffery as his "big brother"—turn things around in his third NFL season. "It's been a blessing. He's like my big brother," Agholor said. "When I was in college, he would shoot me a text to tell me he saw me balling or that I had to do this or that. I took his word."

The mentor role was something that Jeffery gladly took on. It was just a few years ago that he benefited from having a more experienced wideout in veteran Brandon Marshall to learn from in Chicago. "I am very proud of him. I always called him 'little bro.' We have the same agent and all of that," Jeffery said during an interview in the Eagles locker room. "He just has to keep working. He's in here every morning. Now that I am here, I always tell him, 'Yo, you can't let the old head beat you in here.' I always tell him I will be here working. He just has to keep building his confidence and keep grinding."

During the offseason, Agholor began to get back to the 'win each day' mindset that his parents and high school coach instilled in him. Agholor worked diligently to get better at catching the football. He even bought his own jugs machine to have at his house. Agholor continued to train at the Performance Compound in Tampa where he had spent time in the past. While at the facility, he worked with former NFL receivers Yo Murphy and Reidel Anthony.

Former Indianapolis Colts wideout Reggie Wayne was available to mentor Agholor as well. Wayne was someone that Agholor patterned his game after before entering the NFL.

However, it was a meeting with Pro Football Hall of Fame running back Curtis Martin that helped Agholor adopt a new mindset. Agholor started to keep a whiteboard in his locker and wrote quotes on them to remind himself of his mission.

Martin shared a quote with him. The quote was, "When change is necessary, not to change is disruptive."

"You have to remind yourself that if you tell yourself that you are fine, then you can hurt yourself. Things aren't going well for a reason, so you just have to find a way to change," Agholor said.

Agholor seemed to undergo a complete mind transformation during the offseason. He came back to NovaCare Complex for OTAs with a different bounce in his step. He had a much more positive vibe to him. When they hit the field, it was clear that big things were ahead for Agholor. He caught the ball consistently and seemed to be quicker in his routes.

Pederson was pleased with what he saw from Agholor when the team got back together after the offseason. "Nelson's attitude has been great. He's worked extremely hard this offseason," Pederson said during his press conference before organized team activities. "The addition of [wide receivers coach] Mike Groh has really sort of lit a fire with Nelson a little bit, and then the addition [of WRs] Alshon [Jeffery] and Torrey [Smith] and bringing these guys in. As I've said all along, competition, man, sharpens you. And that's what I've seen from Nelson. He's done a great job already this spring."

The additions of Jeffery and Smith presented a challenge for Agholor when it comes to retaining his starting position. But Agholor had a versatile skill set that would allow him to move inside and play the slot as well. With Jordan Matthews nursing an injured knee, Agholor worked with the first team as the slot receiver. He found instant success working inside where there was more space to use his quickness and ability to win at the line of scrimmage. Agholor hadn't been given the opportunity to work from the slot consistently in the previous two years. Ironically, the slot was where an NFC South scout told NFL.com's Lance Zeirlein would be Agholor's best position.

Here's an excerpt from Nelson Agholor's NFL Combine profile on NFL.com: "Right off the bat, his draft value has a ceiling because he's a slot receiver. At least that is how I see it. I don't think he has the speed to get open outside. He's a good value in the middle rounds, though, because of his return-game potential." The scout was clearly wrong to say Agholor had good value in the middle rounds, but he may have been on to something when he projected Agholor to be a slot receiver.

Coach Groh saw the talent that Agholor presented. He just worked to harness it through reworking some of the essential parts of being a wide receiver. "With him, it's going back to basics. Nelson is a first-round pick and has the first-round talent. It goes back to drill work and things that we are focusing on and the way that we train them to simulate a game in everything that we do," Groh said in the spring of 2017.

The drill work that Groh alluded to included a lot of flag work and catching the ball through contact at the top of his route. They focused on getting out of their breaks and getting their head around quickly to locate the football. Groh is a technician when it comes to what he expects from the receivers. He coaches the guys hard and is vocal on reps they take. There was constant coaching on how to refine technique. These things started to become habitual for the receivers, and the results showed.

Agholor caught the ball with more confidence during OTAs and minicamp. He made plays in traffic and the deep passing game and became one of Carson Wentz's primary targets. His confidence began to grow, and it showed in his performance. "Confidence is a result of demonstrated performance. The more positive results that he has in practice that will elevate his confidence," Groh said. "There aren't a lot of slot receivers that can go outside and have success. With his speed and athleticism, he can function at a high level outside, and he looked comfortable inside. He has short-area quickness to allow him to get open against tight coverage. He also has burst and acceleration to get away from defenders. He has a unique skill set."

Heading into training camp, Agholor seemed poised for a breakout season. He had the confidence, consistent showing in practice, and right supporting cast to finally put it all together in 2017. Agholor continued to excel during training camp. He was virtually unguardable in one-on-one portions of practice. Safety Malcolm Jenkins likes to go against who he feels presents the toughest challenges when the receivers and defensive backs have one-on-ones. It was no coincidence that he called out Agholor frequently.

When Jordan Matthews returned to practice, he resumed working with the first team. Agholor was able to still get some reps with the first group, however. The offense looked sharp during training camp. Agholor was making plays, but so was everyone else on the offense. As Agholor began to settle into the role of a slot receiver more, his reps increased. Then the team dropped a bombshell.

The Eagles traded Matthews along with a third-round draft pick in the 2018 NFL Draft to the Buffalo Bills in exchange for cornerback Ronald Darby. Matthews had been one of the most respected receivers on the team. He was considered the leader of the group. Seeing him get traded was a surprise to everyone on the team. It took a toll on the next practice they had. However, they knew the show had to go on.

After practice, Wentz shared what Agholor brought to the slot position and gave him a ringing endorsement. "Nelson has done some good things. He can fly, he can roll in the slot and put some pressure on defenses. They are different skill sets for sure," Wentz said. "He's more of a burner, whereas J Matt [Jordan Matthews] was that savvy possession guy underneath. He made plenty of plays down the field as well. They just bring a different element in the slot."

Agholor had a productive training camp as he geared up for the regular season. The comfort level that he had in catching the football showed every time he snapped the ball out of the air. It became second nature. As a result, he was consistently able to run through the catch instead of slowing down to catch the ball when going across the middle or working out-breaking routes. This allowed Agholor to showcase one of his biggest strengths, yards after the catch.

The season opener against the Washington Redskins set the tone for Agholor and the offense. Agholor posted six receptions for 86 yards and a touchdown. The touchdown came on a broken play in which Agholor turned up the field as Wentz eluded the pass rush. Wentz launched a deep pass that Agholor ran under before making the catch and putting a move on Redskins safety D. J. Swearinger *en route* to the 58-yard touchdown. Philadelphia opened the season with a 30 – 17 win that broke a five-game losing streak to Washington.

Agholor equaled his 2016 touchdown total in the first two weeks of the season after scoring on a nine-yard pass from Wentz against the Kansas City Chiefs in Week Two. The confidence that Agholor played with continued to show in a Week Three win over the Los Angeles Chargers. He had three receptions for 58 yards. One of those catches was a beautiful over-the-shoulder fingertip catch down the sideline for a 36-yard gain.

The game the following week against the Arizona Cardinals gave the home fans a chance to see just how explosive Agholor can be. He ran a deep over route, tracking down a bomb that Wentz threw for a 72-yard touchdown. Once again, Agholor made a spectacular fingertip catch. What was once considered a weakness suddenly became a strength. Agholor was catching everything thrown his way.

Cardinals defensive back Budda Baker tried to tackle Agholor after he caught the ball. A well-placed stiff-arm and a little shake-and-bake topped off with a backward fall into the end zone made the fans at Lincoln Financial Field go crazy.

The way Agholor pulled away from the defender and ran down the ball was reminiscent of what former Eagles wideout DeSean Jackson used to do on a weekly basis. Agholor's touchdown celebration further evoked memories. "That was kind of like a tribute to DeSean Jackson," Agholor said with a smile. "He always used to do that, and I watched a lot of his tapes, so shout out to D-Jax for that."

Having once been a player that had his confidence defeated, it was great to see Agholor play with his newfound swagger. The coaches and players loved what they saw from Agholor. "It's total confidence, and it's—I think it's me believing in him, the coaching staff on offense believing in him, and the players around him believing in him. I see this kid every single day, and the way he walks into the building with confidence. Nothing gets him down. He works extremely hard, and he's playing at a high level right now," Pederson said after the game about the improved version of Agholor.

"That play to Nelson [Agholor] was a huge play. It just shows how far he has come in the past couple years. We are really happy with where he's at, his growth this whole year," tight end Zach Ertz said after the game.

Football was fun for Agholor once again. It was like he was back at Berkeley Prep High School working hard during the week and getting the reward on game day.

Agholor's catch and run ability surfaced against the Carolina Panthers on Thursday Night Football. The Panthers made the mistake of putting linebacker Shaq Thompson in coverage against Agholor. Wentz saw Agholor come open on a slant from the slot position and hit him in stride. Agholor caught the ball effortlessly and accelerated like a sports car, pulling away from the defense for a 24-yard touchdown. In only six weeks, Agholor matched the total touchdowns (three) he had over his first two seasons. It was clear a turnaround was taking place. Agholor scored again the following week against the Redskins to push his total to four touchdowns in seven games.

The Eagles offense spreads the ball around. Agholor seemed to be gaining more and more of Wentz's confidence. The two players seemed to have a knack for connecting on big plays. Agholor shared what helped make them more connected. "Just more reps. In between periods [at practice], if the defense is going and we're not doing scout team, we go on the side, we throw more, we communicate," Agholor said. "He tells me what he sees on film. I'm always asking him questions. And he's a quarterback that allows you to do that. I have a lot of respect for him giving me the opportunity to always stay in his ear. And also calling me over to throw extra routes, and telling me where he wants me to be."

Perhaps the biggest sign of Agholor's turnaround came in Week Thirteen against the Seattle Seahawks. Agholor returned to the scene where he had hit rock bottom a year ago. This time he was determined to leave with his head held high. Agholor exploded for a career-high seven receptions for 141 yards and a touchdown.

He could not be stopped as he ran deep routes from the slot. Wentz was able to step up in the pocket and find him coming open down the field multiple times. Agholor abused former Eagles cornerback Byron Maxwell throughout the game, including a 27-yard touchdown catch.

Even though the Eagles lost the game to the Seahawks, Coach Pederson was proud of the way Agholor was able to turn things around. He had come a long way since the last time they were at CenturyLink Field. "He continued to work, even through the struggles. He continued to fight and battle and show up early and stay late if he had to," Pederson said after the game. "And you just have to go back sometimes, go back to their college days, and show them exactly why they were drafted in the first round or wherever they were drafted and say, 'This is the guy that you are, and you can be.' And you just spend time with him. And then just he himself, just his work ethic every single day, never got down on himself, and fought himself out of it."

Speaking of going back to the college days, the next game for Agholor and the Eagles was in Los Angeles against the Rams. Agholor got to go back to Los Angeles Memorial Coliseum, the site of his standout career at USC. Going back to the Coliseum was something that Agholor really looked forward to. Carson Wentz suffered an injured knee late in the game and was replaced by backup QB Nick Foles. Faced with a crucial third and eight, Foles and Agholor connected on a nine-yard play that gave the Eagles a first down that helped them milk time off of the clock.

Pederson praised the quarterback and receiver for making a critical play that helped lead to a win that secured the NFC East Division title for the Eagles. "For those two to be on the same page like that, that just goes to show you, number one, the route—it was the third play of the game, the same play that we threw the interception on. It's the same route. Nelson learned from that. Nick learned from it," Pederson said. "And that's the confidence that I have to be able to call that play in that situation, third and eight, and know we've got to get nine yards. We executed it, stayed on the field and it helped us win the game."

With Wentz out for the year, Foles was tasked with keeping the momentum going as the Eagles worked towards the postseason. It was going to be up to the playmakers on offense to help him. Agholor showed that he was all-in on helping Foles the following week against the Giants. Foles threw four touchdown passes. One of them came on a remarkable catch by Agholor. The ball was slightly underthrown as Agholor ran a quick fade route, but Agholor was able to jump and take the ball away from the cornerback for the score.

As the Eagles geared up for the postseason, offensive coordinator Frank Reich praised Agholor for the intensity that he brought to the team during practice and how it has rubbed off on others. "His confidence, the juice, the energy he brings to practice, his preparation. It has been relentless, it has been consistent. I think now the next level is it's infectious on other players," Reich explained. "There's always a point in time where if you go through a bad spell, you've got to first kind of defeat the enemy within. Now it goes from, 'Hey, I'm past that now.' What really great players do is they make the players around them better. That's what we're seeing with Nelson."

After clinching the home-field advantage in the playoffs with a Week Sixteen win over the Oakland Raiders, Pederson decided to rest most of the starters in Week Seventeen against the Dallas Cowboys. Having worked mostly with the second team, Foles was still trying to find chemistry with the receivers. But Agholor felt things were settling in as they entered the playoffs.

Agholor had a key play in the divisional playoff game against the Atlanta Falcons. With the offense sputtering, Pederson took advantage of Agholor's running ability and gave him a handoff that ended up going 21 yards giving the Eagles the ball in the red zone. The big gain led to the only touchdown the Eagles scored in the game, which came on a one-yard run by LeGarrette Blount.

Philadelphia won the game 15 – 10 and advanced to the NFC Championship. Agholor had three catches for 59 yards against the Minnesota Vikings in the NFC Championship game. His biggest play was a 42 – yard reception in which he saw Foles step up in the pocket, so he turned his route up the field to uncover himself. The Eagles punched their ticket to the Super Bowl with a 38 – 7 win over Minnesota.

During media night, former Eagles cornerback Eric Rowe was going to be matched up with Agholor in the slot. Rowe said he and Agholor used to battle during practice when they were teammates. Rowe was the Eagles second-round pick after Agholor was selected in the first-round in 2015. He was happy for the progress that Agholor was able to make over the past year. "I see his confidence in his body language, and he's catching the ball. I knew he had it in him. He got that mental block out, and it's really good for him. He gets route separation, he's quick," Rowe said during media night.

Agholor took in the scene during Super Bowl week but kept his focus on the task at hand. The Eagles approached their media obligations with a mindset of just having fun. "I keep the main thing the main thing. This is a great opportunity for us. In our field, this is what we play for. Media, that's part of the game, so I am here to respect that and do what I do," Agholor said. "At the end of the day, I get to go back home, get my rest, watch my tape, and get my recovery so I can go handle my business."

Multiple players on the team came down with the flu during their week in Minnesota. The day before the game, Agholor had to receive an IV. By the time gameday came, Agholor was good to go.

The atmosphere was electric before the Super Bowl. During pregame warmups, Agholor went through his normal routine that included catching tennis balls and running route after route. The stage never got too big for Philadelphia. Agholor finished the game with nine receptions for 84 yards total. He had three receptions for 38 yards on the go-ahead drive. When it mattered the most, he was there for his team. The Eagles had done the unthinkable by beating the New England Patriots 41 – 33 in Super Bowl LII.

The third-year wideout was written off by so many people after struggling over his first two seasons in the NFL. He was called a bust as well as one of the worst draft picks in franchise history. Now Agholor can call himself a Super Bowl Champion. Agholor sat at the podium and thought about how things have played out this year after the game. "You have to work very hard and just make no excuses. That is my recipe," Agholor explained during his Super Bowl post-game press conference. "I can't point the finger at anybody else for last year. That's why I won't point the finger at anybody else for this year either, you know? You just have to work very hard."

It was a long journey for Agholor, but through it all, he continued to push forward. Even though he was the subject of some brutal criticism, now Agholor wants to be a source of encouragement for others who are enduring a tough situation of their own. "I think I am a great example for everybody else who might be going through something similar to what I went through last year. You just have to believe in yourself," Agholor said.

Agholor's middle name is Efamehule. The significance is the meaning, 'May my name never be forgotten.' As an integral part of the first team to bring Philadelphia a Super Bowl victory, Nelson Efamehule Agholor's name will surely never be forgotten.

Player Spotlight: Zach Ertz

Having caught the go-ahead touchdown pass in Super Bowl LII, Eagles tight end Zach Ertz was on top of the world. Ertz came a long way from the days when his toughness was questioned, and he was criticized for not being able to generate a lot of yards after the catch.

What was overlooked was Ertz's sure-handedness and his outstanding route-running. When the 2017 season was all said and done, Ertz took his place as one of the NFL's top tight ends and one of the primary pass catchers in Philadelphia's offense.

It wasn't always sunny in Philadelphia for Ertz. He had to play through injuries and high expectations before he would finally be accepted. The potential that Ertz showed has always been a gift and a curse. He continually faced high expectations because of the flashes of talent he showed since high school. Ertz was recruited to Stanford by former head coach Jim Harbaugh. He was rated as the top tight end recruit in the nation coming out of Monte Vista High School in California.

After redshirting as a freshman, Ertz played in 13 games in 2010, posting 16 catches for 190 yards and five touchdowns. Scoring a touchdown nearly every third time he caught the football showed just what kind of playmaker Ertz could develop into.

Harbaugh packed up and moved on to the NFL, taking over as head coach of the San Francisco 49ers after the 2010 season. David Shaw had served as the offensive coordinator and running backs coach under Harbaugh. He took over as Stanford's head coach after Harbaugh's departure. There was a change at head coach, but under Shaw, Ertz still played in the same scheme. Additionally, he still had quarterback Andrew Luck throwing him the ball along with fellow tight end Coby Fleener.

Unfortunately, Ertz missed three games due to a knee injury that happened during the opening kickoff against USC in October. He returned for the Fiesta Bowl which pitted Stanford against Oklahoma State and had four receptions for 38 yards and one touchdown in a 41 – 38 loss.

Ertz finished the year with 27 receptions for 343 yards and four touchdowns in 2011. With Luck, Fleener, and company declaring for the 2012 NFL Draft, Ertz had to decide whether or not he would return to Stanford or join them. He returned for his junior season and became the focal point of coach Shaw's offensive attack. As a junior, Ertz had 69 catches, 898 receiving yards, and six touchdowns. No FBS tight end had more receiving yards than Ertz in 2012. Ertz was a finalist for the John Mackey Award which is given every year to the top tight end in college football. Despite having worse numbers in every major receiving category, Notre Dame tight end Tyler Eifert was named the Mackey Award winner.

It was time for Ertz to move on to the NFL after his breakout season at Stanford. Entering the 2013 NFL Draft, Ertz was ranked as the second-best tight end prospect by ESPN Scouts Inc and Sports Illustrated. While at the 2013 NFL Combine, Ertz took part in all of the drills. He finished ninth among all tight ends in the 40-yard dash (4.76 seconds).

Later in March, Ertz took part in Stanford's Pro Day and did all of the drills over again to improve his results. Ertz's 40-yard dash time was cut down to 4.67 seconds. He also posted better numbers in the 20-yard dash (2.74 seconds), 10-yard split (1.64 seconds), vertical jump (35.5 inches), and broad jump (9 feet, 6 inches). The Atlanta Falcons and Philadelphia Eagles put Ertz through private workouts before the draft. There seemed to really be a fit for Ertz with the Eagles in head coach Chip Kelly's fast-paced offense. Like a swiss-army knife, Ertz was used everywhere in Stanford's offense. He lined up out wide as a receiver, in the slot, as well as in-line.

Kelly liked to run plays without having the offense huddle up. Everything was up-tempo to keep the defense from substituting. Having a player that can be used in multiple ways such as Ertz would help Kelly and the offense creates mismatches. The Eagles had the number four pick in the 2013 NFL Draft and selected former Oklahoma offensive tackle Lane Johnson with their first-round selection. They had to keep their fingers crossed that Ertz would be around for them in the second round.

Tyler Eifert was the only tight end selected in the first round when the Cincinnati Bengals selected him with the number 21 overall pick. When the Jacksonville Jaguars (SS John Cyprien) and Tennessee Titans (WR Justin Hunter) passed on Ertz, the Eagles pounced, selecting him with the number 35 overall pick.

"What I'm seeing from Chip Kelly is we're going to start defying this offense. Now we've got a detachable H-back tight end that runs great routes," NFL Network Draft analyst Mike Mayock said after the selection.

Kelly had faced Ertz twice while he was the head coach at Oregon. The second time Ertz played against Kelly left a lasting impression. Stanford ended a 10-game winning streak by Kelly's Oregon team. In that game, Ertz had 11 receptions for 106 yards and a touchdown.

"You could never isolate him into one spot, and whenever they got the mismatch he created, he made plays," Kelly told Zach Berman of the Philadelphia Inquirer after picking Ertz in the second round. "I didn't relish coaching against him, and I'm very, very happy that he is on our side now."

Ertz ironically ended up playing for a team that once hosted training camp at the college where his father Doug Ertz played football. Before relocating to the NovaCare Complex, the Eagles used to go to Lehigh University for training camp. The elder Ertz was a fullback at Lehigh in the early 1980s. After graduating from Lehigh and attaining his MBA, Ertz's father got into sales, consulting, and marketing. That helped lead him to the west coast where he is currently the VP of Global Sales for Alameda, California based company Wind River Systems.

Ertz didn't always seem destined to have a football career. When he was younger, he wasn't forced to follow his father's footsteps as a college football player. "We got him involved with a variety of team sports. He played soccer, and then he got into baseball and basketball and was a great swimmer," Ertz's father told *The Morning Call*. "We never pushed him toward football. In fact, his first year of football wasn't until seventh grade. He didn't play in his eighth-grade year, so he focused on basketball," his father said. "That's where we thought he'd end up, playing hoops in college. We never dreamed of the NBA or anything like that, just in college, but then he decided to give football another try."

While he was in high school, Ertz met former San Francisco 49ers All-Pro tight end Brent Jones. He received coaching from Jones, a vital part of the 49ers' Super Bowl victory in 1994. "Brent came in and coached Zach, and he told Zach how good he could be," Ertz's father said. "With that little confidence from Brent, Zach just kept working harder and harder. I had some influence, but Brent and his high school coach, Craig Bergman [a former Santa Clara quarterback], had a much bigger role in getting him to where he is today."

"It was eye-opening. This was a guy that was a multiple-time Pro Bowler helping a kid that was 16 years old telling him what he could be if he stuck to football and worked at it," Zach Ertz said about his conversations with Jones. "I was a basketball player at the time. I really didn't even think about football. I just played to have fun. To have him tell me that I was going to be playing in the NFL if I stuck to it and worked at it, I didn't know what to think at the time. I thought he was crazy. That was the turning point. His direction led me to focus primarily on football. It swayed my mentality."

Things had come full circle with Ertz then in the NFL playing for Chip Kelly, the latest offensive mastermind. Jones had once played for one of football's most trendsetting coaches in the legendary Bill Walsh. Ironically, like Ertz, Walsh had Stanford ties, having once been the head coach there. The Eagles already had veteran tight end Brent Celek on the roster before signing former Houston Texans tight end James Casey to a three-year, $14.6 million deal in March. Ertz was added the following month, giving Philadelphia a well-rounded group of tight ends.

Kelly wanted to use more three-tight end packages to create mismatches against opposing defenses. "We are going to go three tight ends in a game. Now, do they go three linebackers? We split them out and throw passes," Kelly said. "If they go three DB's, we smash you. So, pick your poison. Simple game. Isn't hard. You guys thought coaching was hard. They bring little guys in, you run the ball. They bring big guys in, you throw the ball."

Coming out of Stanford, Ertz was known more for his pass-catching ability. However, the blocking aspect of his game had room for improvement. At six-foot, six-inches and 249 pounds, Ertz had the size to at least get in the way of defenders. In Kelly's offense, tight ends have to be able to fill multiple roles, including blocking, because it is based on being able to run the ball and not have to sub in new packages to do so.

Ertz was aware that his ability to block needed to improve if he wanted to be considered a complete tight end. "I think you see some of these guys like Tony Gonzalez [Atlanta Falcons tight end], Jason Witten [Cowboys tight end], some of those guys being complete tight ends and being huge mismatches in the passing game. I'm really looking forward to showing off what I can do at the next level," Ertz said soon after the draft. "I think one of the tight ends I kind of replicate my game after is Jason Witten just because I think he truly is a really good run blocker as well as a pass catcher. They use him in a variety of ways, and I think the Eagles will do the same with me."

The fact that Ertz wanted to pattern his game after Witten resonated with select media outlets such as NFL.com. They compared Ertz to the former Dallas tight end. When the preseason started, Ertz was behind Celek and Casey on the depth chart. He was also behind them in the pecking order for targets. Gradually, Ertz worked his way past Casey and became the number two tight end on the depth chart.

Player Spotlight: Zach Ertz

Despite Kelly's statements about using three tight end packages more frequently, the Eagles utilized mostly three-receiver sets which resulted in fewer snaps for Ertz. Ertz's first touchdown as an NFL player came in Week Nine against the Oakland Raiders. Shortly after, in Week Thirteen against the Arizona Cardinals, Ertz hauled in five receptions for 68 yards and two touchdowns.

His 68 yards led the Eagles in receiving that week. Ertz's two-touchdown performance was the first time an Eagles tight end had done so since Chad Lewis did so in December 2001. It was also the first time an Eagles rookie tight end scored two touchdowns in a game since Keith Jackson did so in November 1988.

Under Kelly, Philadelphia finished with a 10 – 6 record in both he and Ertz's rookie seasons. The Eagles also captured the NFC East Division title and hosted a playoff game. Philadelphia lost to the New Orleans Saints in the first round of the playoffs by a 26 – 24 score. Ertz gave the Eagles a 24 – 23 lead when he caught a three-yard touchdown pass from Nick Foles, but the Saints were able to connect on the game-winning field goal to move on to the next round. Ertz finished with 36 receptions for 469 yards and four touchdowns as a rookie. It was clear Philadelphia had something special on their hands. Ertz showed flashes of what was to come later in his career.

The future appeared pretty bright for Ertz, especially with Kelly's high-octane offense affording him plenty of opportunities to touch the ball. He was a starter and scored a touchdown in the season opener against the Jacksonville Jaguars. He had three receptions for 77 yards in Philadelphia's 34 – 17 win. The following game saw Ertz post 86 yards on four receptions. He was seeing the field a lot more in his second year. Kelly used three receivers on the field a lot less in favor of having Ertz and Celek on the field more.

Kelly's offense was on a tear in 2014. The up-tempo offense was hard to stop because of the balanced attack that featured LeSean McCoy, who led the NFL in rushing, along with other dangerous receiving options such as Jeremy Maclin (85 rec, 1,318 yds, 10 TDs) who led the team.

Ertz finished with 58 receptions for 702 yards and three touchdowns on 89 targets. He was third behind Maclin and rookie Jordan Matthews who had 67 receptions for 872 yards and eight touchdowns. Matthews was the Eagles' second-round pick (number 42 overall) in the 2014 NFL Draft. He and Ertz were going to be building blocks for the future under Kelly. The two became instant friends when Matthews got to Philadelphia.

Although Ertz finished third on the team in receiving, he set a single-game franchise record against the Washington Redskins in December 2014. Ertz dominated the Redskins, hauling in 15 receptions and going over the 100-yard plateau (115) for the first time in a game. The previous record was held by former Eagles running back Brian Westbrook (14 rec vs. Dallas Cowboys in 2007) and Don Looney (14 rec versus Redskins 1940).

Since 1950, only two tight ends have posted 15 or more receptions in a single game. Besides Ertz, the other tight end to do so was Dallas Cowboys tight end Jason Witten when he caught 18 passes against the New York Giants in 2012. Witten, of course, was a player that Ertz patterned his game after as a young tight end. Having ended the season with a total of 22 receptions for 253 yards in his final three games, Ertz was trending upward when it came to projections for top tight ends in the league.

The 2015 season was another step forward for Ertz individually. But as a team, the Eagles took a step backward under Kelly. Things got off to a rocky start with Ertz missing the preseason after suffering a Grade Three inguinal groin tear. Ertz underwent surgery but returned for Week One.

After having Foles as his quarterback the previous two seasons, Kelly was expected to make a move to trade up to take Oregon quarterback Marcus Mariota in the 2015 NFL Draft. But moving up to one of the top two picks was something that Philadelphia was not able to do.

The Eagles had the 20th pick and stayed put instead of packaging picks to go get Mariota. They ended up selecting former USC wideout Nelson Agholor with the pick. However, Kelly did bring a new quarterback to Philadelphia, former first-round pick Sam Bradford. The Eagles delt Foles, along with a fourth-round pick in 2015 and a second-round pick in 2016, to the St. Louis Rams in exchange for Bradford and a fifth-round pick in 2015.

Ertz was burdened with developing chemistry with a new quarterback under center. The missed time made it difficult for Ertz and Bradford to get their timing down. After a bit of a slow start, Ertz was able to set career highs with 853 yards on 75 receptions, finishing second on the team in both categories. Once again, a late-season hot streak helped boost Ertz's stats. Ertz continued to insert his name into the Eagles' records. His 30 receptions over the last three games of the season set an Eagles record for the most catches over a three-game span. In Week Sixteen, Ertz hauled in 13 passes for 122 yards against the Redskins.

He became only the fourth NFL tight end since 1960 to have multiple games with 13 or more catches and 100 or more yards. The feat put Ertz in some pretty rare company, joining Witten (four), former Browns tight end Kellen Winslow Sr. (three) and former Kansas City Chiefs/Atlanta Falcons tight end Tony Gonzalez (two). Having accumulated a total of 450 receiving yards in the final four games of the 2015 season, Ertz joined Jimmy Graham as the only NFL tight ends with at least 450 yards over a four-game span since 2013.

Ertz was a clear beneficiary of playing in Kelly's offense. That's not to say he wouldn't be productive in others, as he showed later in his career. It was just that Kelly's offense facilitated plenty of targets to go to the tight ends.

After going 6 – 9, Kelly was fired before the 2015 season concluded. Some of the players said there was a disconnect between Kelly and the locker room. Ertz didn't have such a problem, maybe it was because his approach was different. "I've been around unapproachable coaches before. I don't need a best friend as a coach," Ertz said when asked about Kelly. "I need someone that's going to push me to be the best I can be, and that's all I can ask for. I want a coach that's going to maximize my potential," Ertz continued. "That's all you can ask of a coach. I don't really care how that happens. I want to be the best player I can possibly be, and I think a coach helps you along that journey."

The time that Ertz spent with Kelly was going to have an impact on him in the future as a player. Kelly was big on sports science, introducing things such as sleep tests on players, as well as personal GPS tracking during practice, and individualized shakes for each player. Some of these concepts still exist in the NovaCare Complex under Doug Pederson.

"I think everyone's learned a lot from the off-the-field portion of Chip's program. Things I'm going to take with me for the rest of my career, just staying on top of your body, staying on top of your sleep. Things that make sense. Your body is your job, essentially, at this level, and I think the better you can take care of your body, the better you're going to be," Ertz explained.

With Kelly out of the picture, the Eagles hired Pederson to take over as head coach. Pederson offered a return to the days of Andy Reid, whom Kelly replaced. The Eagles wanted more of a player's coach, which is exactly what they got in Pederson. The West Coast offense that Pederson brought with him was a good sign for Ertz.

As a player, Pederson spent time with the Packers and Eagles among other teams. Green Bay liked to use plenty of two-tight end sets when Pederson was a backup quarterback there. That was where he developed an appreciation for 12 personnel, or what he refers to as the 'tiger,' package. Having a piece like Ertz to move around makes the package even more impactful.

"It creates match-ups. If he's an athletic guy, like a Zach Ertz, we can move him around, spread him out. He's good in space and understands a spatial awareness," Pederson said during a press conference after selecting tight end Dallas Goedert in the second round of the 2018 NFL Draft. "He's great in man-coverage because he can separate at the top of the route. Those become big bodies on smaller bodies. Those are the match-ups that we try to create through game planning and through studying our opponents. That's what having two tight ends, we call it 'tiger personnel' on the field allows us to do."

It was clear that Ertz was a significant part of Pederson's offense. Pederson had found plenty of success as an offensive coordinator with the Kansas City Chiefs before coming to Philadelphia. While in Kansas City, tight end Travis Kelce became the focal point of the Chiefs offense under Pederson and Reid. Ertz was poised to take on a similar role to Kelce's for Pederson with the Eagles. But Ertz saw something in Kelce's game that he wanted to improve upon.

"Kelce and I are very different players, but the roles could be similar. I think Travis is a very good player," Ertz said. "Our games are a little different. He's very good after the catch. That's something that I am trying to improve on."

Before what was going to be his final year under his rookie contract, Ertz agreed to a five-year contract extension with the Eagles. The deal was worth $42.5 million, including an $8 million signing bonus, $21 million guaranteed, and an average annual salary of $8.5 million.

Knowing he was going to be in Philadelphia for years to come was something that Ertz cherished. The passion of fans and how deeply they bleed their team's colors is different on the East Coast. Ertz loved their passion and let them know by posting a message on his website.

I love Philly. My family loves it. I love how passionate Eagles fans are about their football, how they live and breathe it. I put a lot of pressure on myself to be the best, and our fans want us to be successful as much as we want to be successful.

What I love more than anything is that fans here in Philadelphia are truly honest with you. If you're not playing great, you're going to hear about it. If you're losing, you're going to hear about it. If they're not happy, they're going to let you know.

I have no issue with that. I know when I'm messing up, and when I do, I feel the same way they do. In life, you have to be accountable. You reap what you sow. When we're playing great and winning, our fans are the best fans in the world, and there's no one else in the league I'd rather play for.

Ertz was finally in a position to start the season with the same quarterback that he ended with the previous year. "I am excited to have the opportunity to have the chemistry with Sam [Bradford] grow. He missed all of OTAs last year," Ertz said in April before the draft. "I missed all of training camp, so our first real action together was game one at Atlanta on Monday night."

In preparation for the upcoming season, Ertz and Jordan Matthews spent time with Bradford at his home in Oklahoma. The trio had big plans for their first season under Pederson. Unfortunately, their plans never came to fruition. The Eagles orchestrated a series of moves to get into position to select North Dakota State quarterback Carson Wentz with the number two selection in the 2016 NFL Draft.

Bradford was dealt to the Minnesota Vikings for a first-round pick in 2017, a week before the season started. Wentz was named the starter for Week One despite only playing in the first preseason game. The continuity that Ertz was looking to experience with Bradford was taken away like a thief in the night. Now Ertz had to turn his attention to building chemistry with Wentz.

Wentz had endeared himself to the veterans because of how he came in and worked hard, knowing he was going to be the future cornerstone of the Eagles. Ertz and many of the other pass catchers were impressed with Wentz's big arm as well as his athleticism. "Guys are confident with him, I think the playbook expands a little bit because he's more of an athlete than some of the quarterbacks we've had in the past," Ertz said.

"We talked about him extending plays. He knows where we are going to be. We haven't repped it much, but you have to go out and make plays for Carson. We have to go out there and get to those spots and make plays."

The season opener against the Cleveland Browns gave Wentz a chance to work with Ertz and the other receivers in live action for the first time. Wentz completed the first regular-season pass of his career to Ertz for a 14-yard gain on the first drive.

Ertz was knocked out of the game in the first half after lowering his shoulder along the sideline as he tried to gain extra yards. He was diagnosed with a rib displacement near his left shoulder. The displaced rib posed a risk to cause further harm because it was in the upper portion of Ertz's body, near his neck. The rib had become displaced underneath Ertz's collarbone. Before the injury, Ertz had five receptions for 68 yards.

Pederson decided to play it safe and place Ertz on a day-day-day status. Ertz missed the next two games but had the benefit of the bye week to recover from his injury. Once Ertz returned, he struggled to have an impact because he and Wentz couldn't get on the same page. Ertz only had one reception in back-to-back weeks against the Redskins and Minnesota Vikings.

The Eagles mounted a late comeback against the Redskins, but the drive stalled when Wentz and Ertz couldn't connect on a slant from Washington's nine-yard line. Philadelphia would have been able to draw even if they could have scored a touchdown on that play. The pass sailed a bit on Wentz as he released it causing Ertz to have to reach up to snag the pass. The high pass caromed off Ertz's hands and fell incomplete. Many fans and media types questioned Ertz's heart for not making the catch. However, a high throw is the last thing any pass catcher needs when coming across the middle where defenders are lurking and waiting to deliver a punishing hit.

Wentz knew he needed to get a better throw to Ertz so he can snatch the ball out of the air and get into the end zone. "I had to get it down. I threw it high on him and made it hard on him, but if I get it down and put it on his chest, it's a walk-in touchdown, so it's something we have to clean up," Wentz said after the game.

The stretch of games with minimal production was getting to Ertz, but he kept his cool and patiently waited for his time to get more targets. He was confident the opportunities would come. "Being a competitor, you want the ball in your hands. I am not trying to overwhelm him [Carson Wentz], he has so much other stuff that he has to worry about. I talk to Chase [Daniel], and he will relay it to Carson if he sees the same thing. I am just not trying to put pressure on him right now," Ertz said after practice in October.

"You can't really put the message out there in the first place. Otherwise, it will come off as selfish. My job is to get open and make plays when the ball is in the air and block when they ask me to block. I think I've done that the last two games, but the ball has not come my way."

Ertz and Wentz stayed after practice regularly to work on routes and getting more familiar with each other. Wentz knew he had to get the chemistry down with his tight end. Once they were able to do so, the results followed. "Throughout the last couple of weeks, there have been things that he and I have been working on quite a bit. We'd stay after practice and try to clean up the timing and things, so it's always a good thing to get him involved," Wentz said before their Week Nine game.

Offensive coordinator Frank Reich felt like the two were going to get connected soon. He saw the work they put in to get on the same page. "We need to keep trying to get the ball to him and have a breakthrough in one of these games. We need to get him the ball. He's a great tight end," Reich said during his weekly press conference. "It's easy to have a natural connection with Ertz. He's such a good route runner, and he understands leverage, how to get open. Those two should hit it off, and we need more production so we will keep fighting for that."

Ertz caught eight passes for 97 yards against the Giants in Week Nine which was at that time a season-high. That number increased to nine receptions against the Cincinnati Bengals in Week Thirteen.

Even though those nine receptions resulted in 79 yards and a touchdown, Ertz's toughness was questioned once again in the Bengals game. The play that everyone focused on was a block Ertz didn't make.

Wentz broke the pocket and scrambled before cutting to his right towards the sideline. Bengals linebacker Vontaze Burfict was closing in on Wentz just before he stepped out of bounds. Ertz had an opportunity to lay a big hit on Burfict, but it seemed like he got out of the way at the last second rather than take the kill shot. "I understand how it looks on the film," Ertz said at his locker the Wednesday after the game. "I won't get into the details as far as what happened on the play. I'm focused on getting better. Maybe I could have impeded [Burfict's] progress a little more to ensure that he didn't get closer to Carson on that play."

There were questions about Ertz's heart for not delivering the hit. The belief was that Ertz was playing soft because he wanted to avoid getting injured. That didn't sit well with Ertz. "If you go on the field worrying about getting injured, you're going to lose as soon as you step on the field," Ertz said with a scowl. "For someone to think that I am not playing hard because of a past injury . . . I don't focus on injuries. Everyone has had them in this league. I am not injury-prone by any means. I am not in the business of preservation by any means. I am in the business of winning football games."

But it could also be said that Ertz made a smart play by avoiding what may have been viewed as an illegal crackback block on a defenseless player. At the end of the day, the reason for not taking the shot is something that only Ertz will know, but his offensive coordinator at the time stood by him. "The block was a nonfactor in the play. Sometimes you get a shot like that, and you take it. I have learned over the years to trust the players' instincts," Reich said.

Reich had to revisit the issue after the season opener in 2017. He offered an even more passionate defense of his soon-to-be All-Pro tight end. "I remember after the Cincinnati game, there were multiple questions about him being aggressive. I've never questioned Zach in that regard. Zach plays to win! Zach is a winner! He runs his routes aggressive, he's aggressive to the ball. I have never thought anything other than that," Reich said emphatically. "I played with a lot of great players who will step out of bounds rather than take a hit when they know they got the first down. Barry Sanders, he never took a hit on the sideline. Nobody called him a coward. You have to be smart too."

Getting blown out 32 – 14 by the Bengals certainly didn't help matters. It was a disappointing loss that Philadelphia had to put behind them. Not only was Ertz's heart being questioned, but Pederson was also being doubted as a leader because of the poor performance that week. The Eagles had lost three games in a row, and someone had to take the heat.

Ertz bounced back the following week by posting 10 receptions for 112 yards against the Redskins. They lost the game, but Ertz showed that he won't allow adversity to negatively impact his performance. "He wanted to sort of redeem [himself] and get back out on the field and do what he can do," Pederson said at his postgame press conference. "Obviously I thought he did a nice job."

After the game, questions about redemption from the previous week were abundant. Ertz took the high road when answering them. "Everyone deals with adversity in different ways. I am not going to let one play define my career—good or bad," Ertz said at his locker after the game. "Obviously, there was a lot of hoopla surrounding that play last week, and I just wanted to tell my teammates that I got their back regardless of what is going on, on the outside. I was focused on being the best tight end I could be today and being the best teammate I could be. I think I did that today."

Things started to click just a little too late for Ertz and Wentz. As the season wound down, Ertz came alive for Philadelphia. Over the last two months of the season, Ertz caught 63 passes from Wentz. It was the second most in the NFL over that span. Green Bay Packers wide receiver Jordy Nelson was the only player to have more receptions (66) in November and December. The grand finale was a 13-catch, 139-yard performance in a 27 – 13 win over the Dallas Cowboys at Lincoln Financial Field. Ertz scored two touchdowns in the game.

"I mean I think it's just reps upon reps, feeling confident with one another," Ertz said after defeating Dallas. "I'm in the spots where I'm supposed to be, and he's throwing the ball where he's supposed to throw it. And it's just finally starting to click for us. It was huge for us, we want to build momentum going into the offseason."

Ertz had finally become that safety net that Wentz looked to when things have gone awry. Earlier in the year, wide receiver Jordan Matthews was that guy, but now Wentz had more than one option that he trusted.

"He [Ertz] is a heck of a player. He creates mismatches all over the field. So it's just been one of those things, when things break down or when I know I need somebody, Ertz has been that guy. He's has been that guy that steps up for us," Wentz said after the game. "So it's been really good working with him. Along the same lines, I'm looking forward to continuing that relationship and building that chemistry down the road."

Ertz led the Eagles with a career-high 78 receptions for 816 yards and four touchdowns. His 78 catches were the second-most ever by an Eagles tight end, behind only Keith Jackson (81 in 1988). There was no reason not to think that Ertz would elevate his game even further with another year in Pederson's scheme and with Wentz as his quarterback. The table was set for a true breakout season, but that was what had been said over the past two years.

Former Broncos tight end and Hall of Famer Shannon Sharpe heaped praise on Ertz and called for Pederson to make him a bigger part of the offense. "There's no doubt that his talent is undeniable," Sharpe said. "He can make plays. He can run after the catch. I love what I see from him. When Zach gets hot, he's catching ten, eleven, or twelve balls a game."

Before the 2017 season started, Ertz married his long-time girlfriend Julie Johnston, an American soccer player and FIFA Women's World Cup champion.

During the offseason, Wentz and the receivers worked on refining specific situational parts of the passing game. One of the areas they worked on was finding ways to take advantage of broken plays. They worked the QB scramble drill and set rules in place to dictate where the pass catchers would go given any particular way Wentz had to move within the pocket and extend the play. Ertz praised Wentz for his sometimes Houdini-like ability to elude pressure and extend plays. He said it gives the offense an advantage because defensive backs are not used to being in coverage for an extended time.

"When you have an athletic QB like Carson, the ability to extend plays stands out," Ertz said during a press conference before the 2017 NFL Draft. "Having a full offseason, you're able to talk about scramble rules as an entire offense. We weren't as detailed in our scramble rules because the whole group has never really been together. That's something that we have to take advantage of. Huge plays can happen in those scramble situations."

When training camp rolled around, Ertz and Wentz were already in full swing. The two put on a show in front of the media with Ertz catching plenty of passes across the middle. Ertz also showed how he could attack the ball, catching passes from Wentz along the sideline on corner routes as well as deep down the field on posts. The defense countered by putting safeties in coverage against Ertz, but that still didn't matter.

The offense was dominant during the first part of training camp. They signed free agent Patrick Robinson in the spring, but he struggled. Something had to change. As a result, Jordan Matthews, one of Ertz's closest friends, was sent to the Buffalo Bills along with a third-round draft pick in exchange for cornerback Ronald Darby.

The move rocked Ertz and Wentz because the trio of players had grown very close over the course of last season. Ertz came to Philadelphia one year before Matthews. They were friends since 2014 when Matthews was drafted.

"If it weren't for the Philadelphia Eagles, a kid from Huntsville, Alabama and a kid from California would have never met," Ertz explained. "He has a brother for life in me, and he knows that."

Trading Matthews meant Ertz was going to be the clear-cut favorite target for Wentz. The team had signed top-level free agent wideout Alshon Jeffery, but Wentz still had to develop a rapport with his new receiver. Ertz was now going to get more opportunities in the slot as well. Agholor took over duties as the primary slot receiver, but he and Ertz presented different challenges to defenses.

The success at the end of the 2016 season was carried over to the season opener the following year. The Eagles went to Washington and gave their division rivals a beatdown, ending a five-game losing streak to the

Redskins. Ertz picked up right where he left off in December by catching eight passes for 93 yards. One of Ertz's catches came on a 3rd & long when Wentz extended the play and Ertz turned his route up the field to get open for his quarterback. It was exactly what they had worked on during the offseason. And it resulted in a critical first down late in the game.

"We have scramble rules that we put them in all summer," Ertz said after the game. "It's kind of just seeing what he sees and trying to see the game the same way. It's impressive what he's able to do in the pocket. You have to love a guy that can extend the play like that."

After a loss to Andy Reid and the Kansas City Chiefs in Week Two, Ertz and the Eagles hosted their division rivals from the North. The Giants came to town looking to hand Philadelphia a loss in the home opener. Giants safety Landon Collins got a taste of what Ertz brings to the table as a rookie in 2016. Collins had a lot of respect for Ertz, but he planned to prevent Ertz from having an impact.

"He's a competitor, always going a hundred and ten percent. He's proved why he should be one of the highest-paid tight ends," Collins told ESPN before their matchup. "Every time I lined up against him, he was giving it to me, and I had to make sure I gave it back. His route-running isn't superb, but he gets open somehow, and he has great hands. He goes up and attacks the ball, not letting it fall into his hands so that a DB can make a play on it."

Collins didn't stop there.

"I think it's going to be a better matchup. Just hope I don't get too many push-offs from him at the top of the route. His breakdown isn't that good in the hips, so he tends to push off, and that's how he gets open most of the time. If I can get away from that and deflect those push-offs, I can get a bead on him and make some plays." The plan worked to an extent. Ertz still posted eight receptions but for only 55 yards. He scored his first touchdown of the season, however.

The 2017 season saw Ertz get off to the best start of his NFL career. Through the first four games, Ertz had 326 yards and a touchdown—that's 106 more yards than in the first four games of any other season in his career.

The injury bug resurfaced for Ertz once again in 2017 when he suffered a strained hamstring in practice before their Week Nine game against the Denver Broncos. He missed the game but was back for their showdown with the Dallas Cowboys in Week Eleven after the Eagles' bye week.

Ertz's best game came the following week when he posted 10 receptions for 103 yards and a touchdown against the Chicago Bears. He was really starting to come into his own as a tight end. Every week Ertz gave the Eagles a mismatch when they had the ball. Reich grew more and more confident in Ertz as the primary target in Philadelphia's offense. He loved the way Ertz was able to get open against opposing defenses. In 10 seasons as a coach, Reich has worked with premier tight ends such as Antonio Gates (Chargers) and Dallas Clark (Colts). He felt that Ertz was working his way towards that kind of impact.

"Zach has the rare ability to bend, and he has the subtle movements that are hard to defend. He is elite in just his route-running skills and his footwork and his body movements and the way he can bend," Reich said.

"You can't even explain it. There are certain routes that we run that if I were coaching a receiver, I'd coach him to run 'this' route a certain way to beat the defender playing 'that' leverage. Zach will run it, not in a completely different way, but in a way that I just wonder how did—his feet did something that I'm not used to seeing on that route. I don't understand how he did that. He has instinctive traits, and I think he has that in spades. I mean, the guy is unbelievable."

Ertz suffered a concussion in a Week Thirteen game against the Seahawks while catching a pass across the middle. The concussion held him out of the following week's showdown with the Rams in Los Angeles.

After being cleared for the Week Fourteen game against the Giants, Ertz scored his final touchdown of the season. It was Ertz's eighth touchdown of the season which tied him for the second-most in a single season for an Eagles tight end, behind Pete Ratliff's 10 touchdowns in 1965.

One of the players that Ertz patterned his game after was Cowboys tight end Jason Witten. Before what would be Witten's final game in the NFL, he gave a ringing endorsement of Ertz. "I think he's just an exceptional player. Love how he plays the game, the position. It's good to see him having the year that he's had and develop into his own, one of the best in the game," Witten said. "They've had a huge amount of success this year offensively, and I think a large part of it is his part of his ability with good route-running to finding the soft spots in zones—all the things that make up tight ends. He's done a really good job with the play-action that they've done and taken advantage of that."

Ertz continued his dominance in the postseason. He was a key part of a blowout win over the Minnesota Vikings in the NFC Championship, catching eight receptions for 93 yards. The fifth-year tight end was named to his first Pro Bowl in 2017. Despite being voted in as a starter, Ertz had to bypass the game for a bigger cause—to play in the Super Bowl.

During the 2017 season, Ertz and Eagles fans connected. Fans appreciated how Ertz worked diligently to become a better blocker and an all-around better football player. Like he said when he signed his contract extension before the 2016 season, Ertz appreciated the fans for their passion and outspokenness.

One of the things that really endeared Ertz to his fans happened after the NFC Championship game. Zach Ertz's wife Julie is a member of the US women's national soccer team. She was not able to attend the NFC Championship Game because she had some business of her own to handle. The US team was playing their season opener against Denmark in San Diego. She scored a goal in their victory. Julie was overcome with emotion when she found out about her husband's team advancing to the Super Bowl. A local media person showed Ertz a video of his wife's reaction.

Ertz said his wife was the first person that he thought of when the final seconds ticked off the clock. He knew she was on the other side of the country playing a game of her own, which made him proud. "I wish she was here. It's tough not having her here. I can't wait for her to be back," he said as he fought back tears.

"I wanted to cry, too, honestly. We had just beat the Vikings in the NFC championship game—and it started to sink in that we were going to the Super Bowl and I could barely keep it together," Ertz said in a journal entry for The Player's Tribune. "More than anything, I just wanted to call my wife. So after I hugged some teammates and took in the confetti, I sprinted straight to the locker room to FaceTime Julie."

During the week leading up to the Super Bowl, Ertz spoke about how, despite having the best record, no one picked the Eagles to go far and how it fueled them to prove everyone wrong. "We've had a chip on our shoulder the entire year. No one picked us at the beginning of the year. No one picked us after Carson got hurt," Ertz said during media availability. "No one picked us first round, second round, the NFC Championship. We're just excited to be here, the chip on our shoulder will never leave. I think being in the NFL, you have to have one."

Ertz made sure his team did more than just play in the Super Bowl. He helped seal the deal when he made the play of his career came in Super Bowl LII against the New England Patriots. With 2:21 left on the clock, Ertz lined up out wide on the left side of the formation. There were three receivers to the opposite side which drew most of the defense.

Rookie running back Corey Clement went in motion to the right out of the backfield and one of the Patriots' defenders went with him. The Eagles now had Ertz matched up one-on-one against the safety. Ertz ran a slant and made his break inside as the safety fell. Quarterback Nick Foles saw him and delivered a strike, hitting Ertz in stride before he dove into the end zone for the go-ahead score. When Ertz hit the ground, the ball came out, but he secured it as he rolled over onto his back. The play was under review, but the officials confirmed that it was a touchdown.

Philadelphia held on to beat the Patriots 41 – 33 thanks to two defensive stops, one of which was a strip/sack of Tom Brady by Brandon Graham.

After the game, Ertz looked back on the emotional rollercoaster he had been on over the last two years. He thought about the fans and how so many of them stuck with him through tough times. "I told them at the time that they would never question my effort again, and I am lucky to be in this situation playing for this city. I will never take it for granted. I love them because the fans never gave up on me," Ertz said.

"Thank you guys for everything this year. You guys have been longing for this," Ertz shouted from the stage as he hoisted the Lombardi Trophy. "We are lucky to be here and deliver this for you guys. . . . We are world champions!"

Player Spotlight: Brandon Graham

With just over two minutes left in Super Bowl LII, the Philadelphia Eagles were protecting a five-point lead. Future Hall of Fame quarterback Tom Brady dropped back to attempt a pass.

Eagles defensive end Brandon Graham had moved inside to defensive tackle in Philadelphia's NASCAR package. Graham got a tremendous jump off the ball and managed to get under the right guard as fellow defensive end Chris Long collapsed the pocket from the outside. Brady was left with nowhere to step up, and Graham got a hand on him as he attempted to deliver a pass to avoid being sacked. In the process, Graham made Brady fumble, and the ball bounced right into the hands of rookie defensive end Derek Barnett who was coming from the other side. Philadelphia had thwarted Brady's attempt to work his late-game heroics. Graham celebrated with his defensive teammates as the Eagles offense came onto the field.

The game wasn't over yet. Kicker Jake Elliott nailed a 46-yard field goal to give Philadelphia an eight-point lead over the New England Patriots. Brady had one last attempt to mount a comeback, but his last try fell incomplete as the last seconds ticked off the clock. The Eagles had done the unthinkable and Graham's sack-strip went down as one of the biggest defensive plays in Philadelphia sports history.

After the game, Graham looked back on the play of his career. "I knew I had a one-on-one with the guard. I knew he liked to be aggressive, so I tried to act like I was pulling. I snatched it right off, and Tom Brady's arm was right there, and I went for the ball," Graham explained from the podium. "I had the one-on-one all game, I've been bulling him, and I switched it up. I acted like I was going to bull him and snatched him. Tom Brady's arm just happened to be there, and I swiped. And I didn't even realize I got it until I saw Derek Barnett pick it up and I just knew we had less than two minutes to go, and I was just so thankful to be able to make that play to get us off the field and change the game."

The moment of euphoria after becoming Super Bowl Champions was something that many Eagles fans had been longing for, having waited over 60 years to see their team win it all. For many of them, the idea of having Brandon Graham be the one to help seal the deal was something they would have never thought of a few years ago.

Graham was selected by the Eagles in the first round of the 2010 NFL Draft with the 13th overall pick. To acquire the number 13 pick, Philadelphia traded picks number 24, 70, and 87 in the 2010 Draft. Given their need for a safety, it had become a foregone conclusion that former Texas defensive back Earl Thomas was going to be the pick. Thomas was considered to be the top safety prospect in 2010. Philadelphia fans were starving for another star at the position after Hall of Fame safety

Brandon Graham

Keith Allison

Brian Dawkins had been allowed to leave via free agency before the 2009 season. To the dismay of many Eagles fans and the surprise of various draft analysts, Graham was the pick. The Seattle Seahawks selected Earl Thomas with the next pick.

Eagles fans were upset about Graham being on their team before he even set foot on the field. Graham had been a late riser thanks to an outstanding performance during Senior Bowl week in Mobile, Alabama. He capped it off by being named the MVP of the Senior Bowl game with five tackles, two sacks, and one forced fumble. Before the Senior Bowl, Graham had made a name for himself as a defensive end at Michigan.

While at Michigan, Graham first started to carve his niche as a versatile defensive lineman. Graham played both defensive end and defensive tackle for the Wolverines as a freshman. He was named team MVP in back-to-back years to finish his career at Michigan. He had five tackles for a loss against Ohio State in his final college game.

Graham carried the momentum from his performance against the Buckeyes to the Senior Bowl and to the NFL Combine in Indianapolis after that. At the NFL Combine, Graham ranked eighth among defensive linemen with a 4.72 40-yard dash and tenth in the bench press with 31. The senior defensive end had done everything he needed to thrust himself into the first round of the NFL Draft. It was just a matter of where he would go.

On a rare occasion, a number 54 Eagles jersey with Graham's name on the back can be spotted during games at Lincoln Financial Field. Anyone wearing that jersey is a true fan of Graham's. That jersey means someone stuck with him from the start. When Graham first got to the Eagles, he decided to wear number 54. He eventually changed his mind and decided to wear number 55, the same number he wore at Michigan.

Graham agreed to terms on a five-year $16.8 million contract in July 2010. He reported to camp ready to go and notched his first sack in the preseason against the Cincinnati Bengals. When the regular season started, Graham was behind veteran defensive ends Juqua Parker and Trent Cole on the depth chart. Graham's first regular season sack came against the Detroit Lions in Week Two of his rookie year. He registered sacks against the San Francisco 49ers and Chicago Bears to give him three sacks as a rookie.

Graham's rookie season came to an end when he suffered a torn ACL in Week Fourteen against the Dallas Cowboys. He was placed on injured reserve in December, and one week later had micro fracture surgery on his right knee. The recovery from his injury caused Graham to be placed on the active/physically unable to perform list in July just before training camp in 2011. Graham was taken off the list and returned to practice in October before making his debut against the Bears in Week Nine. The 2011 year was not kind to Graham. The injury slowed him down, and at that point, he hadn't lived up to the expectations that many had for a first-round pick.

When 2012 came around, things got off to a hot start for Graham. Now fully recovered from the knee injuries, Graham was able to show what he could do. He posted 3.5 sacks in the preseason. As the season went on, Graham's snaps increased. Graham had 5.5 sacks on the year, including a 2.5-sack performance against the Bengals in Week Fifteen.

Fans saw the performance that Earl Thomas was showing for the Seattle Seahawks and started to grumble about how Thomas should have been the Eagles' pick in 2010 instead of Graham. Thomas and the Seahawks started to form a young secondary that was making a name for themselves. The third-year safety had five interceptions as a rookie and two in 2011. While Graham had 5.5 sacks in Philadelphia in 2012, Thomas posted three interceptions the same year, including one that was returned for a touchdown. Fans started to call Graham a bust because they felt he didn't live up to his draft status.

Defensive end Jason Pierre-Paul was selected two picks after Graham and had 16.5 sacks in 2011 followed by 6.5 in 2012. To make matters worse, the Eagles were getting further and further away from the team that was a perennial contender for most of Andy Reid's tenure as head coach.

Chip Kelly took over as head coach of the Eagles after a 4 – 12 season led to Reid being relieved of his duties. Kelly brought defensive coordinator Billy Davis with him to Philadelphia. Davis had been well-versed in the 3 – 4 defense, which meant Graham was going to have a position switch. Instead of playing defensive end and being able to rush the pass in addition to setting the edge against the run, Graham was now asked to add pass coverage to his assignments. The move required Graham to think a lot more about each snap he played. There were more keys to read which slowed him down as a pass rusher.

Despite being a four-year veteran, Graham didn't start any games in 2013. He ended up with only three sacks as well. It became clear that Graham needed to start showing traces of the talent that caused him to be one of the top defensive line prospects in 2010. The question was, is it in the right system?

Graham accomplished a life milestone when he married Carlyne Williams, his high school sweetheart, during the offseason in 2014.

Player Spotlight: Brandon Graham

While Graham was at Michigan, Carlyne was at Lane College, where she graduated *cum laude* earning dual degrees in criminal justice and sociology in 2008.

Graham started to show life in 2014 but only started one game. By this point, he had started to settle into the outside linebacker role that he occupied in Billy Davis's 3 – 4 defense. Graham had 5.5 sacks in 2014 and displayed in spurts how he could be a disruptive player. This came even more into focus for Graham in 2015.

The Eagles saw that Graham had potential as a player and wanted to make sure he was with the team for the upcoming years. Graham came close to signing with the New York Giants but settled on a four-year, $26 million deal to remain in Philadelphia.

The Giants wanted to pair Graham with Jason Pierre-Paul, a fellow 2010 draft pick. "It was serious [with the Giants]. I told them I was serious, but I'm going with the Eagles. I couldn't go up the street. I couldn't be this close to Philly and think I was not going to have to watch my back around the New York area. It's too close," Graham said at his press conference after signing a new contract with the Eagles.

The major factor for Graham to stay in Philadelphia was getting an opportunity to be a starter. He had been trapped behind team leader Trent Cole for quite some time on the depth chart. Cole signed a free agent deal with the Indianapolis Colts which opened things up for Graham to take over in Philadelphia.

"Give me the opportunity to show that I can be the starter for this organization, and be pretty good at it, too," Graham said. "[Cole's departure] helped out in the decision. I love Trent to death, and we still talk every day, but I understood when Trent was here, he's a great player. "He's been here longer than me. They love him. But as soon as he wasn't here, I knew that was my opportunity, and [coach Chip Kelly] showed me that he was going to give me that opportunity."

Armed with a new contract and more playing time, Graham started 10 out of 16 games in 2015. He posted 6.5 sacks on the season and started to show more often how he can be disruptive player. Chip Kelly was fired after going 6 – 9 with one game remaining. Gone was the 3 – 4 scheme that caused Graham to be switched to outside linebacker.

Graham shared some of the things that he felt went wrong under Kelly. "It was all of the crazy stuff that happened," Graham said. "You have Maclin, you have McCoy, you have D-Jacc, all of them were gone. I think that is what hurt. They were good guys. When those guys left, it was hurtful. They were friends. I am not going to say they gave up. A lot of people felt some type of way."

The players seemed to feel alienated from their head coach when Kelly was there. Team owner Jeffrey Lurie wanted to get back to the kind of coach that would be more relatable for the players. In came Doug Pederson, a disciple of former Eagles head coach Andy Reid and a former Eagles quarterback. Pederson immediately injected a family-type atmosphere in Philadelphia.

"Coach Pederson is taking an active role and making sure he speaks to everybody," Graham explained. "All I want to be able to do is communicate with my head coach, say hello, have side conversations. Now everything is laid back. Everybody is talking to everybody. Everybody is excited to get to the season and show what we have been working on."

Pederson brought Jim Schwartz with him as the defensive coordinator. Schwartz was one of the coaches that Graham worked with during his display of excellence at the Senior Bowl in 2010. "I had Jim at the Senior Bowl. He is intense and will get the best out of everybody. He isn't scared to challenge you," Graham said during locker room availability in the spring of 2016. "I'm excited, you look at his top defenses with the Bills; he's had some good defenses that really get after it."

The 4 – 3 defense that Schwartz used focused on getting pressure with the front four. The defensive ends positioned themselves in a 'wide-nine' alignment which means they lined up on the outside shoulder of the offensive tackle. They're able to simply pin their ears back and go after the quarterback. This was a good fit for a player with Graham's skill set.

Schwartz viewed Graham as a player that was meant to play his defensive scheme. "There's a lot of things that he brings to the table. He's strong," Schwartz said. "He's hard to handle on the edge. Sometimes that lack of height that he has that some people think is a disadvantage he can use to his advantage."

Schwartz feels the so-called weakness can actually be a strength for Graham when he goes against bigger left tackles. He singled out two of the best pass rushers over the last 10 years as examples of how to make being undersized work for them. "I think of some guys in the history of the NFL: Dwight Freeney is one, Dumervil too," Schwartz said. "Those guys that sometimes you get those six-foot-seven offensive linemen, they have a hard time handling those six-foot-one, six-foot-two type guys. They have a little different leverage, and it gives them a different look. I think Brandon could bring some of that."

Graham said he went extra hard in the weight room during the offseason. The new scheme gave him extra motivation. During the offseason, Graham also found another source of motivation when he and his wife Carlyne welcomed a baby girl, Emerson, to their family before the 2016 season.

"The preparation and work during the offseason helped," Graham said. "I took it to another level. Having a daughter this offseason, everything became viewed a different way."

Led by Graham, the defensive line showed how they would be a force to be reckoned with during live periods of practice in training camp. They dominated during inside run, which is a competition of the offensive line and a running back versus the defensive line and linebackers. The Eagles' offense had trouble getting to the end zone during live team periods that focused on goal line situations as well. The tone was definitely set for the defensive line to be the heart of Philadelphia's defense.

Graham opened the season with a sack in three straight games. The pressure that he put on the quarterback helped the Eagles start the season with three consecutive wins. "For me, now all I have to do is worry about going after the quarterback. I am happy to be back to the four-three and able to attack the quarterback not having to worry about coverage too much," Graham said. "As an outside linebacker standing up, you see too much. You want to be everywhere."

Graham said his path to the quarterback was slowed down because of how he had to read his keys as an outside linebacker in the 3 – 4. There were times that he had to drop back into coverage and other times where he had to set the edge. That was no longer the case under Schwartz.

Despite Graham's fast start, he ended up with 5.5 sacks on the season. However, it was more than just sacks that showed how disruptive he was. Graham regularly got into the backfield and put pressure on the quarterback. Although he didn't always get to opposing quarterbacks to register the sack, Graham still forced a hurried throw that knocked off the timing of opposing passing games.

Throughout the season, Graham continued to draw praise from his defensive coordinator. "He's a good player. Not only is he a good player, but he plays with incredible effort and toughness," Schwartz said at his Thursday press conference before a Week Eleven game against the Seattle Seahawks. "He is very conscientious, rarely makes mistakes. I can't say enough good things about him. If I played in the NFL, I'd hope I could play as good as him."

Graham's leadership role became more evident in his first year under Doug Pederson. He was the player, along with safety Malcolm Jenkins, that drew the biggest media scrums at his locker after practice.

During the 2016 season, wide receiver Nelson Agholor was going through tough times. Like Graham a couple of years before, Agholor was a first-round pick that was struggling to live up to his draft status.

"I've been through what he's been through," Graham said. "I called myself a bust at one point. A guy came to me and told me to never say that again and said to keep my head down and keep working. That's what I will say to Nelson, 'Keep working, don't worry about it, not everybody knows the work that you do.'" That was sound advice for Agholor and came from a 'been there, done that' perspective.

Graham's leadership was on display off the field as well. He started the Team Graham 55 organization which has a goal 'to make positive changes and influences, one community at a time.' Graham's organization hosted the 15th annual "Bowl with the Birds" event in Cherry Hill, New Jersey.

"I'm just happy to be able to give back because changing somebody's life is why we're here, and why we do what we do," Graham said.

Community service truly resonates with Graham's family because of his wife, Carlyne's background and her story. "My wife was adopted, and she was in the system, but she was not a product of her environment. She went out there and got three degrees," Graham said. "Without people helping her, she probably would have never got out of her situation."

Before moving to Philadelphia, Carlyne was a case manager and a director of social services serving families in the Chicago area. After Carlyne graduated from Lane College, she furthered her education by earning dual degrees in social work and child and family law from Loyola University (Chicago).

The 2016 season was a building block in many ways for Graham and for the Eagles. While they finished with a 7 – 9 record, it was clear that big things were ahead for them. Graham was named a second-team All-Pro after the season. He was perhaps the best run defender on the Eagles. Graham's high motor was on display as he chased down ball carriers on the opposite side of the line. Graham set the edge aggressively, forcing running plays back inside.

Player Spotlight: Brandon Graham

The vibe was different after the 2016 season. There was a winning culture in place which was forged from a tough year that included a five-game losing streak. However, the locker room stuck together this time.

"It starts with coach [Doug Pederson] and us as leaders make sure we police a lot of things," Graham said at his locker after the final game of the 2016 season. "You have to look at yourself first before you give criticism. No one ever wavered, no one blamed each other. Everybody came to work every day. He's straight up. He will shoot you straight and let you know the real. You can trust a guy like that. He played fourteen years, and he understands where we are. He talks to guys and wants to get to know who's here. He does a lot of great things. That's always a great start."

The 2017 season was a time for Philadelphia to take things to the next level. The Eagles added to their defensive line by signing free agent Chris Long and selecting former Tennessee defensive end Derek Barnett with the 14th overall pick in the draft.

Before voluntary OTAs, a report surfaced that Graham was not going to report because he wanted a contract extension. Eagles Executive VP of Football Operations Howie Roseman spoke about Graham on 94WIP FM. He said Graham has not told him that he intends to hold out. "He has personally not done that," Roseman explained on the Angelo Cataldi Show. "Brandon's been unbelievably positive about his role on this football team, being here, and I don't get any dissatisfaction from him."

Roseman would not get into any details about Graham's contract or whether or not Graham's agent Joel Segal contacted him about a new contract. Graham posted a message on Twitter to clear the air.

Back in Philly and I just wanted to clear a few things up for all of our fans. I was never holding out. I was in Detroit last week spending some time with my family.

I love playing in Philly. I love our fans, and I love this organization. I've never had an issue with my contract. I don't know where that news came from. I will be at OTAs leading the charge and ready to get things started.

Graham knew that he had to be a leader in 2017 more than ever. He made his presence known as soon as he walked into a room. You could always hear Graham coming before you saw him because his loud voice commanded attention.

"I know a lot of people are looking at me to be a person to say things to get things rolling," Graham said during a media session at the beginning of offseason workouts. "I've got to make sure in those moments when somebody needs to step it up, as far as being a leader or saying something, I want to make sure that I embrace that role and be comfortable in those moments to be able to speak."

Graham instantly took to rookie defensive end Derek Barnett. Coming out of Tennessee, Barnett had drawn comparisons to Graham because of their ability to get a jump on the snap and their similarities when it comes to size. Graham had a rough start to his career. Fortunately, he had a veteran in Trent Cole to give him guidance as he made the tough transition into the NFL. Having benefited from Cole's veteran presence, Graham was ready to pay it forward to Barnett.

The veteran worked closely with Barnett, giving him pointers on technique and helping him develop the right mindset when it comes to coaching. "Just watching him, telling him what I see that he does well," Graham explained. "There are things that coach is trying to coach him on that I had problems with. I try to show him better ways of doing certain things just until coaches feel comfortable and trust you, then you can kind of do your thing a little bit on top of what coaches want."

Graham set it in his mind to increase his sack totals. He had gotten close to the quarterback multiple times in the past, but this year his focus was on finishing the job. "My next step is to get off the ball a lot faster. Last year, I wasn't getting off the ball as consistently as I could have," Graham explained on Sirius XM NFL Radio. "That's the separation from having five and a half sacks to having fifteen and a half sacks. There are a lot of times where I am one step away, but I could have gotten off the ball a lot faster."

The focus on getting a better jump on the snap showed during training camp. Graham found himself getting the upper hand against the Eagles' offensive linemen. To keep their veteran leader happy, the Eagles front office added some performance incentives to Graham's contract that gave him the potential to earn another $1.5 million.

The season opener saw Graham have his impact right away. Graham crashed down the line and tackled Washington Redskins running back Chris Thompson on the opposite side of the line for a loss on the second play of the game.

"We wanted to set the tone early and create our own identity on what we will be this year," Graham said after the game. "There are a lot of guys here from last year, and we wanted to show who would make that jump in year two."

Player Spotlight: Brandon Graham

Graham finished with two sacks on the day, including a sack-strip that defensive tackle Fletcher Cox scooped up and returned 20-yards for a touchdown. The Eagles stopped a five-game losing streak to the Redskins thanks to a 30 – 17 victory on the road.

After a Week Two loss to the Kansas City Chiefs, Philadelphia ripped off a nine-game winning streak. Things were really looking good for the Eagles, and people started to believe they could make a run in the postseason. Graham had set a career high with seven sacks through 12 games. He felt the work ethic that had been established in Philadelphia would help the team go far. In his mind, it's all right to occasionally picture reaching the ultimate goal.

"Just keep reminding ourselves," Graham said. "Because sometimes it feels good to look ahead and be like, 'Oh, man, I feel like we've got the Super Bowl team.' And I do feel that way because of how we work. That's how I kind of judge it—off of how we work and how we prepare when we're playing against an opposing team."

Unfortunately, the win streak ended with a loss on the road against the Seattle Seahawks in Week Thirteen. Graham had 1.5 sacks in the game, however, and pushed his total to 8.5 on the year. His best play of the game came when he lined up at defensive tackle. Graham got to quarterback Russell Wilson and brought him down, which was something that many defenders struggled to do.

Moving inside to tackle put Graham against former first-round pick Luke Joeckel. Graham exhibited incredible strength by throwing Joeckel (six feet, six inches, 306 pounds) into a rushing lane to keep Wilson from being able to step up in the pocket. Graham explained how he made the play after the game.

You have to make sure you capture the gap first. Once you see him turn his shoulders, you have the option to go outside or inside. It depends on which way you feel once you get in that position up the field.

Once he [guard Luke Joeckel] put his hands on me, I lifted one of them off and pressed and stabbed him with the other hand. That kind of got him off balance as I pulled him. I pulled him up the field, and he turned as I pulled him.

I was able to come back inside, and Russell Wilson happened to be right there. I threw Joeckel where Wilson usually escapes, outside. I threw him outside, and I played inside so that he couldn't escape.

It was all a feel. I felt like Joeckel jumped out at me so I was able to get inside, pop his hand off and throw him the way he was going and it ended up working out.

Next up was a trip to Los Angeles to face the Rams and their high-scoring offense. The Eagles went directly to Los Angeles from Seattle and spent the week in Costa Mesa before the game. While they were on the West Coast, many of the players were joined by their families. Graham took his wife and daughter to the National Ice Cream Museum in Los Angeles.

The Rams game presented one of the biggest tests for the Eagles in 2017. They held on to win the game but lost quarterback Carson Wentz for the season due to torn knee ligaments. Nick Foles came on in relief, and Graham sealed the deal by returning a fumble 25 yards for a touchdown giving the Eagles a 45 – 35 win. The win clinched the NFC East Division title.

Graham had a sack the following week against the Giants. That gave him a total of 9.5 sacks for the year. His goal at the beginning of the season was to post double-digit sack numbers. With a 10-sack total staring him in the face, Graham wasn't able to get to Raiders quarterback Derek Carr and bring him down the following week against the Oakland Raiders on Christmas Day.

The NFL announced their Pro Bowl rosters during the week leading up to the Raiders game. Six Eagles players were named to the Pro Bowl, but Graham was not.

"I just have to put that extra chip on my shoulder and keep working hard. It's all about the numbers," Graham said with a smile. "When you are voting, all you see is the sacks. I get it. I just have to get more. They went right down the list in numbers. I understand. All this does is put a bigger chip on my shoulder for next year."

The defensive ends that made it ahead of Graham include Chandler Jones (17 sacks) of the Cardinals, DeMarcus Lawrence (14.5 sacks) of the Cowboys and Everson Griffin (13 sacks) of the Vikings. It's no coincidence that these defensive ends have the top three sack totals in the NFC.

Although he was disappointed in not being named to the Pro Bowl, Graham was instead focused on going to a bigger bowl, one that would be played in February. Graham tweaked his ankle in the Raiders game and missed practice before the season finale against the Dallas Cowboys. The time off allowed Graham to rest his ankle sprain but kept him from getting another shot at adding to his sack total. It's very likely that Graham would have been able to get a sack against a Cowboys' offensive line that had struggled for most of the year.

However, it was more important to have Graham ready for the playoffs. The Eagles had clinched home-field advantage in the postseason. Playing in front of the fans at Lincoln Financial Field gave the Eagles the boost they needed to hand the Atlanta Falcons a 15 – 10 loss in the divisional round of the playoffs.

During his press conference before the NFC Championship game, Graham gave props to the fans for coming out to support and invited them to do so once again. "Oh man, I can only imagine because last week, it exceeded my expectations and it's only going to get even better," Graham said. "I'm just excited, man, because I know we going to bring the energy and I know the fans going to bring the energy and have a Championship Game here for all the marbles, to go to the Super Bowl. I know it's going to be electric."

The Eagles weathered the storm caused by an early score by the Minnesota Vikings. Philadelphia scored 38 unanswered points *en route* to a 38 – 7 win over the Vikings to earn a trip to Super Bowl LII against the New England Patriots.

When the Eagles spoke at the Super Bowl media night, the big question was how they would hold up against the mighty Patriots. Graham wasn't buying into the mystique of the Patriots, but he also made sure he paid attention. "Anybody can be beaten. We are all human. You just can't beat yourself when you are playing these guys," Graham said. "They don't beat themselves often. They do a great job of preparation and keeping their team together. We are similar. We all strive, we have good chemistry together, and it's all about who executes the best."

Super Bowl LII had a different setting since it was in Minnesota. Due to the frigid temperatures, many of the players from both teams frequented the Mall of America. Their hotels were attached to opposite ends of the mall, but they ran into each other as they walked around the mall to shop and visit restaurants. That was something new to Graham and helped stoke his fire leading up to the game.

"Seeing those guys in the mall makes me ready to go play right now," Graham said. "You don't usually see your opponent during the week until it is time to get to the stadium and play. You have to continuously tell yourself, 'Get your mind off football' but when it's time to practice, practice but don't overdo it."

By the time game day came for the Eagles, they were ready to unleash on New England. They came out to local artist Meek Mill's song, 'Dreams and Nightmares,' which was when it became evident just how charged up Philadelphia was for the game.

The Eagles scored first and took an early lead, but Brady and the Patriots came roaring back to start the third quarter. After a series of back and forth touchdowns being scored, Philadelphia was desperately in need of a stop. That was when Graham made the play of his life. Up to that point, there had been no sacks in the game by either defense.

The premier pass rushers have a knack for making a play when it is needed the most. Graham did just that when he rushed New England quarterback Tom Brady from the defensive tackle position and managed to get the sack-strip. It was a tremendous play that was a timely turnover giving the Eagles offense a chance to extend their five-point lead with less than two minutes left in the game. When the time expired from the clock, the city of Philadelphia had their first Super Bowl champions.

Graham was at the podium after the game with his daughter sitting on his lap. She sang 'Fly Eagles, Fly' as Graham talked about how the team stuck together all year. "I think when a lot of guys went down, it was just more so about us. Next man up, next man up. We just had a bunch of guys that couldn't wait to get that opportunity, and when they did get that opportunity, there wasn't no drop off," Graham said. "I think with us it started with Howie [Roseman] and those guys making the right choices, bringing the guys in that jelled well with us. Our chemistry was outstanding this year, and it was just all about us in that room. All year we didn't have nobody going or saying nothing in the media, going crazy saying, this is what happened, blaming people. We just took it on the chin, and we fixed it, and now these are the fruits of our labor right here, our hard work."

It was fitting that one of the plays that had so much to do with the outcome came from a defensive player. The Eagles as an organization have always been known for their defense. Players such as Chuck Bednarik, Reggie White, Jerome Brown, and Brian Dawkins come to mind when thinking about the best players in franchise history. Graham made sure to give the past players a shout out. One of the players that he thought about first was his mentor Trent Cole.

"T-Cole is the first one that was calling my phone when I got up in there. That's who I talked to before the game too. I wanted to thank him.

Player Spotlight: Brandon Graham

I mean, at that point, they paved the way for us. T-Cole, he helped me become a pro," Graham said.

During locker cleanout on Wednesday, Graham said, "All of the former players, that was for them. They have been in this battle and know how hard it is to get there, and I am just happy to get over the hump for them."

Player Spotlight: Nick Foles

To the average American, an insurance policy is a necessity, but it is also something they would rather not have to use. For the Philadelphia Eagles, their insurance policy on the 2017 season was bringing quarterback Nick Foles back to be the backup to franchise cornerstone Carson Wentz.

Executive VP of football operations Howie Roseman was already on the hook for $4.1 million of Chase Daniel's 2017 salary despite the fact he was not on the team. Still, Roseman went out and signed Foles to a two-year contract worth $11 million before the team reported for 2017 offseason workouts.

As a second-year quarterback, Wentz was expected to take a giant leap in 2017. A part of that leap was to not always be willing to put his body in harm's way so he can avoid injury. It was hard for Wentz to scale down his aggressive style of play that at times can be considered reckless.

Coming from a small-school, Wentz had some question marks from the media about the level of talent he played against. A lot of media types were quick to say number one pick Jared Goff was the more NFL ready prospect because he went to California and played in the PAC-12.

However, it was Wentz that was more ready to contribute right away because unlike Goff, he played in an NFL-style offense that used a lot of West Coast concepts. Playing at North Dakota State, where he was asked to make checks at the line of scrimmage before the snap and change protections on any given play, gave Wentz a taste of what he would be asked to do at the next level.

Wentz was thrust into action as the starter in 2016 just a week before the season kicked off. Veteran quarterback Sam Bradford was supposed to be the starter, but he was dealt to the Minnesota Vikings in exchange for a first-round pick in 2017.

Head coach Doug Pederson did a good job of bringing Wentz along as a rookie. He ended the year with 3,782 yards and 16 touchdowns. His 14 interceptions that year put a black eye on his stat line. Entering the 2017 season, there were certain things the coaching staff worked to get better at. These improvements started with the quarterback.

"Situational football is a big part of winning games in the NFL. There were times where Carson wasn't so great in situational football as a rookie," QB coach John DeFilippo said before training camp. "He logs things in the back of his memory. He's not what I call a 'repeat offender.' He's not going to make the same mistake twice."

The situational football improvements that DeFilippo desired included being more efficient in the red zone, converting on third downs more frequently, and protecting the football. Although these measuring points fall under the category of a team stat, they are some of the most telling when it comes to determining how good a quarterback is. Wentz was challenged to improve in these areas so he could take his game to the next level.

Staying out of third-and-long played a big role in improving the third down efficiency. The Eagles were able to get better in these situations by taking advantage of Wentz's athleticism which helped when the play broke down. Wentz was a dynamic playmaker when he was able to break out of the pocket and scramble with his eyes down the field. The wide receivers and tight ends were perfectly in sync with Wentz which allowed them to uncover themselves for big plays.

The timing was especially dangerous with tight end Zach Ertz. Ertz has dealt with multiple quarterback changes over the years. But he was more than excited to have the security of Wentz with him for years to come. "With Carson, we know who our quarterback will be for the next ten years," Ertz said. "I am excited about finally having the same quarterback, having the whole offseason and being able to get into the fine details about the route-running with him, how he sees things, how I see things based on certain coverages."

As they continue to work together, Ertz wants his connection with Wentz to be viewed along with some of the top QB/TE tandems in the NFL. "If you look at the great tight end/quarterback relationships in this league, whether it be Tom [Brady] and Gronk [Rob Gronkowski], Drew Brees with Jimmy [Graham] when they were together, even Cam [Newton] and Greg [Olsen], those guys had been together for a long time," Ertz explained. "When you are on the same page and you know when a defense gives you this coverage, you know exactly what you are going to do and when to expect the ball against certain coverages. It's that constant camaraderie to where one person knows what the other is going to do without even thinking about it."

Philadelphia's focus on converting third down opportunities paid dividends in 2017. They finished in a tie with the Buffalo Bills for the top NFL team on third downs converted, averaging 6.4 per game. Remarkably, they converted more per game (7.4) on the road than they did at home (5.5). The Minnesota Vikings narrowly edged the Eagles in third-down conversion percentage per game. Minnesota converted on 44.72 percent of their third-down opportunities while the Eagles converted on 44.69 percent.

Nick Foles

The red zone efficiency was something else they had to improve upon entering the 2017 season. Wentz needed to become more accurate when it came to ball placement in tight windows. During training camp, the offense spent extended parts of practice focusing on the red zone. Things become a lot tighter inside the 20-yard line. There is a lot less room for the receivers to run routes and less ground for defenses to have to protect.

That is why executing with surgeon-like precision is a must in the red zone. Wentz improved drastically in ball placement. He consistently delivered the ball in the strike zone (top of the jersey numbers to the facemask) on slants and other routes across the middle. The passes were much easier to catch in traffic because of how well Wentz put them on the pass-catchers. Wentz also threw with more accuracy on out-breaking routes such as speed outs when he needed to anticipate the receiver making his break and have the ball there for the wideout to catch as he comes out of the break. The touch on corner routes was much better. Wentz started to drop the ball just over the pass-catcher's shoulder allowing him to get his feet in bounds and secure the catch.

The Eagles finished third in the NFL averaging 2.2 red zone touchdowns per game. Only the New England Patriots and Los Angeles Rams finished ahead of Philadelphia. The Jacksonville Jaguars (68.9 percent) were the only team that finished ahead of the Eagles (64.0 percent) in red zone scoring percentage in 2017. This was the result of yet another focus during the offseason.

Finally, the third area for improvement that was connected to Wentz was limiting turnovers. As a rookie, Wentz threw 14 interceptions. The coaching staff wanted Wentz to be more careful with the football. A large part of that involved his accuracy on deeper in-breaking routes such as dig routes and dagger routes. At least six of Wentz's 14 interceptions in 2016 came as a result of the ball sailing on him. He wasn't following through on his throws and oftentimes he didn't step into his throws as much which limited the velocity he was able to put on the ball to get it to his pass-catchers.

Wentz worked on these areas and suddenly the Eagles offense took off. One of the biggest beneficiaries was wide receiver Nelson Agholor. Agholor is an explosive player once he gets the ball in his hands. Given how Wentz threw with better timing and precision on the slants, digs, arrows, daggers, and other routes, the interceptions from 2016 turned into big plays and touchdowns in 2017. The 14 interceptions from the previous year were reduced to seven.

Wentz increased his touchdown pass total from 16 touchdowns as a rookie to 33 touchdowns in 2017. The 33 touchdown passes set a franchise record for touchdowns in a single season. Wentz was now drawing MVP consideration. He set the franchise record in Week Fourteen against the Rams, but it came at a high cost. The second-year quarterback tore multiple ligaments in his knee and was done for the season.

Wentz attempted to dive into the end zone for a touchdown late in the third quarter during Philadelphia's 43 – 35 win over Los Angeles in a showdown that pitted 2016 NFL Draft number one pick Jared Goff against Wentz, the number two pick. The fact that he came back on the next play and threw the touchdown added to the already immense respect Wentz's teammates had for him.

"He's a battler and he's a warrior. You see it time and time again. The guy is never fazed by anything. Guys kind of expected him to be out," tight end Zach Ertz said about Wentz after the game. "We didn't see [the hit], but we heard about it from the sideline and we heard that it was pretty bad. We were asking around in terms of how Carson was doing, and he was right back out there throwing and everyone was kind of taken aback by it. It just kind of shows the love that he has for his teammates. He never wants to let us down and that's why guys love playing for him."

Player Spotlight: Nick Foles

Remember that insurance policy that Howie Roseman and the Eagles took out before the season when the Eagles signed free agent quarterback Nick Foles? Now it was time to cash in.

Foles entered the game with the Eagles down by four points at the start of the fourth quarter. It was his first game action since he appeared in mop-up duty against the Chicago Bears in Week Twelve. He completed his first pass of the game on a throw to Alshon Jeffery for a 10-yard gain. A 10-yard run by Jay Ajayi got the offense in scoring position as Jake Elliott kicked a 41-yard field goal to pull Philadelphia to within one point.

The Rams fumbled at their own 25-yard line on the following drive. Foles completed three consecutive passes to set up another field goal by Elliott to take give the Eagles a 37 – 35 lead. Foles's biggest play of the game came on a third down with eight yards to go for a first down. Nelson Agholor ran an out-breaking route from the slot and Foles hit him perfectly for a nine-yard completion that gave them another set of downs.

The first down caused the Rams to use their second timeout and allowed the Eagles to run the clock down to seven seconds left in the game on the ensuing plays before punting to Los Angeles. Defensive end Brandon Graham recovered a fumble and returned it 16 yards for a touchdown to give the Eagles a 43-35 win and clinch the NFC East Division title.

After the game, head coach Doug Pederson endorsed Foles and assured everyone that he felt the Eagles could still win with him under center. "Nick has played a ton of football. I was here when we drafted him, and we drafted him for a reason. Then we went out and got him again this off-season for a reason," Pederson said. "You never want it to be under these circumstances, but at the same time, my confidence is extremely high in Nick."

The moment wasn't too big for Foles thanks to his previous experience. He was ready to go when called upon and takeover for the rest of the season. But, he hated that it came as a result of Wentz suffering an injury. "I'm absolutely ready, I mean that's why I'm here. I'm ready to go. Prepare every day, work every day, so I'm ready to go if need be," Foles said after the game. "It's emotional for me. I work with him every day. We do everything together. I'm excited we won, but at the same time, I'm dealing emotionally with seeing him go down. You never want that."

Getting his first significant action as an Eagles quarterback in a game that came against the Rams was ironic. Foles was traded along with a fourth-round draft pick in 2015 and a second-round pick in 2016 to the Rams in 2015 in exchange for Sam Bradford and a fifth-round pick in

2015. Foles signed a two-year, $24.5 million extension with the Rams in August of 2015. What seemed like a fresh start turned into one of Foles's worst seasons as a pro.

After throwing four interceptions against the Green Bay Packers in Week Five, Foles was benched in favor of backup quarterback Case Keenum. Foles ended up being the starter once again two weeks later after Keenum suffered a concussion, but he continued to struggle. Three interceptions against the Cincinnati Bengals and an interception against the Arizona Cardinals landed Foles back on the bench when Keenum recovered from his concussion and was able to return to the field.

The Rams moved from St. Louis to Los Angeles and traded up to the number one pick in the 2016 NFL Draft to select Jared Goff. Foles asked to be released and the Rams obliged by cutting ties with him on July 27, 2016.

An old friend came calling when Foles was on the open market. Former Eagles head coach Andy Reid was in charge of personnel when Philadelphia selected Foles in the third round (number eighty-eight overall) of the 2012 NFL Draft. Foles signed with the Kansas City Chiefs soon after being released by the Rams. It would come out later that at that point, Foles was contemplating ending his NFL career.

The solo season in St. Louis with the Rams took a toll on Foles. Once he cut ties, he took a fishing and camping trip with his brother to clear his mind. While he was on the trip, he called his wife and talked with other family members about what was next. Foles also prayed on it.

"You go through a lot of emotions. Changing teams, being traded, going there, going through that year, and once I was a free agent, we just sort of sat there and said, 'Hey what do we want to do?'" Foles said as he looked back on the tough time. "It was the first time I had been a free agent in my career and it was the first time I had to make a decision because I was drafted and traded. I was leaning toward not playing and stepping back."

The decision to keep playing was his conclusion and he knew Andy Reid was the coach that would present the best situation for him. According to NFL Network's Ian Rapoport, Foles also had offers from the Dallas Cowboys and Minnesota Vikings. Reuniting with coach Reid was easily the best decision for Foles.

"He's a man that has always believed in me, no matter what has gone on in my career," Foles said. "He drafted me. I knew that if I played for him, I'd give it one more shot -- that he could find the joy. If I had joy in there, he could bring it back out, and he sure did."

Player Spotlight: Nick Foles

Foles signed a one-year deal worth $1.75 million. The deal also had an option for 2017 that would have been worth between $6.75 million and $16 million depending on how well Foles played in 2016. As a backup to Chiefs starting quarterback Alex Smith, it was not likely that Foles would play a lot. However, Foles did get a chance to play when Smith went down with a concussion in Week Eight against the Indianapolis Colts.

He finished the game having completed 16 of his 22 pass attempts for 223 yards and two touchdowns. Foles got his only start with the Chiefs the following week against the Jacksonville Jaguars. Kansas City won by a score of 1 – 14 and Foles finished with 20 of 33 pass attempts for 187 yards and a touchdown.

The Chiefs declined the second-year option on Foles's contract, making him a free agent. Foles knew exactly where he wanted to go after becoming a free agent again. The Eagles were intrigued when they saw Foles hit the open market. Head coach Doug Pederson reached out to Foles about returning to Philadelphia.

Signing Foles was a move that everyone was on board with. One of the biggest supporters was team owner Jeffrey Lurie. "We made such a concerted effort to make sure we could get Nick [Foles] back on the team. We prioritized more money for the second quarterback position than most any other team in football," Lurie said about bringing Foles back. "We even were willing to eat a lot of the contract we had so we could go out and get Nick. We've always had so much confidence in Nick. His Rams experience we thought was an outlier. He's a wonderful person and we knew he would be great with Carson."

Things had come full circle for Foles. He was back in Philadelphia and back with his former position coach, Doug Pederson. The relationship that Foles and Pederson have can be traced back to Pederson's early days in the NFL as a coach. He played a large part in the Eagles selecting Foles in the third round of the 2012 NFL Draft.

"Coach Pederson is the one who drafted me. He was the only coach who flew down to Texas and worked me out," Foles said after the NFC Championship Game against the Vikings. "I was only worked out by one team, and that was by Coach Pederson. Coach Reid and the Philadelphia Eagles took a chance on me. To win this game for him and this organization is something very special."

As a former quarterback, Pederson was able to really dig in and get to know Foles during the pre-draft visit. Because he was the only coach to visit Foles, there was plenty of individual time to see what Foles brought to the table.

"He reminded me after the game last night that I was the only coach to go work him out as a player," Pederson said during his Monday press conference after earning a trip to Super Bowl LII. "It goes a long way to his confidence and my confidence in him. To be able to separate and come back together now and do the things that we've been able to do is a credit to him."

Foles was a backup to quarterback Michael Vick when he first got to the NFL. He made his NFL debut against the Dallas Cowboys when Vick was removed from the game with concussion-like symptoms. He threw his first career touchdown pass against the Cowboys. It came on a 44-yard pass to wide receiver Jeremy Maclin. He finished with 22 completed passes out of 32 attempts for 219 yards, one touchdown, and one interception.

Vick was ruled out of the next game in Week Eleven against the Washington Redksins, leading to Foles getting to make his first start. Despite Philadelphia's 31 – 6 loss to the Redskins, Foles was 21-for-47 in passing with 204 yards, along with no touchdowns and two interceptions.

After Vick missed the next three games, Andy Reid named Foles the permanent starter regardless of when Vick was cleared to return. Foles made Reid's decision look like a brilliant one in his first game after taking over as the team's starter.

Foles threw the ball 51 times and completed 32 of his passes including two touchdowns. One of the touchdowns was the game-winner as time expired, sealing the deal for Philadelphia's 23– 21 win over the Tampa Bay Buccaneers in Week Fourteen. The Eagles lost their next two games with Foles as the starter. In Week Sixteen against the Redskins, Foles broke his hand resulting in his placement on injured reserve and ended his season.

He finished his rookie season having thrown for 1,699 yards in seven games. Foles had six touchdown passes and five interceptions. With Foles on the shelf, Vick was the starter in the season finale. The Eagles suffered a 42 – 7 loss to the New York Giants and ended the season with a 4 – 12 record in 2012. It seemed like Andy Reid's time with the Eagles ran its course and a change was needed.

Reid was fired after the season and Chip Kelly was brought in to rejuvenate Philadelphia's stale offense. Kelly had been known for his high-scoring offense at Oregon. Vick and the Eagles agreed on a one-year restructured contract worth up to $10 million. They also selected USC quarterback Matt Barkley in the fourth round of the 2013 NFL Draft.

Kelly announced that Vick, Foles, and Barkley would take part in a three-man competition to be the starter. The 2013 battle primarily came down to Vick versus Foles, with Vick being named the starter in late August.

Despite being named the backup, Foles committed to staying ready if an opportunity came up. He first saw action in Week Four against the Denver Broncos and completed three out of four attempted passes for a total of 49 yards and one touchdown, with no interceptions.

A couple of weeks later, Vick suffered a hamstring injury against the Giants and Foles entered the game again. Foles completed 16 of 25 passes for 197 yards and 2 touchdowns, leading the Eagles to a 36 – 21 win over New York. The hamstring injury kept Vick from being able to play the following game. Foles got the start and began to tip the scales in his favor.

The second-year quarterback took advantage of the extra playing time against the Buccaneers. He connected on 22 of 31 passes for 296 yards and was accountable for four total touchdowns (three passing, one rushing) in a 31 – 20 win over the Bucs.

The NFL named Foles the NFC Offensive Player of the Week for his performance against Tampa Bay. The high of Week Six was followed by a low in Week Seven against the Dallas Cowboys. Foles struggled to find a groove in the game, completing only 11 of 29 passes for 80 yards. A head injury knocked Foles out of the game, and rookie Matt Barkley got under center while he was out.

Foles was unable to play the following week due to a concussion which coincided with Vick's return from a hamstring injury. Against the Giants, Vick aggravated the injury and had to leave the game. When Week Nine rolled around, Foles was clear to return and got the start against the Oakland Raiders. He delivered a historical performance that day.

Against the Raiders, Foles threw for seven touchdowns which tied him for an NFL record. He became one of three quarterbacks to throw seven touchdowns and zero interceptions. For the second time in 2013, Foles was named NFC Offensive Player of the Week Award after his performance which was summed up by a perfect QB rating of 158.3.

"I'm really proud of what he's doing. You go out and set a record, and there's nothing like that, man. It's a day you'll never forget," Vick said of Foles's game against the Raiders. "Twenty years from now, when you're talking about Foles in the record books—him and Peyton Manning—I can tell my kids, 'I was at that game.'"

Things started to really take off for Foles after the Raiders game. He completed 12 out of 18 passes for a total of 228 yards, three touchdowns, and no interceptions the following week against the Green Bay Packers. His passer rating skyrocketed for the second consecutive week, finishing at 149.3. Foles became the first quarterback in NFL history to post passer ratings above 149 in consecutive weeks.

Foles led the Eagles to three consecutive wins in November. Philadelphia entered the bye week with a 6 – 5 record and suddenly tied for first place in the NFC East. Chip Kelly named Foles the permanent starter during the bye week. Foles received the NFC Offensive Player of the Month award for his stellar performance in November.

Coming out of the bye week, Foles completed 21 of 34 passes for a total of 237 yards, with three touchdowns and no interceptions against the Arizona Cardinals. The Eagles held off a late comeback attempt by the Cardinals and won 24 – 21.

"He's the starting quarterback for the next thousand years here," Chip Kelly jokingly said the day after the game. "You know, so, I hope Nick [Foles] is here for a long time. I'm a big supporter of him, I think he does a fantastic job, but we also know that injuries occur in this game and that's why I always qualify what I say. I love the kid and I think he's playing outstanding."

It was clear that Foles was totally dialed in. Foles set a team record for most passes without an interception (233). The record was previously held by Vick (224). He also moved within one touchdown pass of the record 20 straight touchdown passes set by Peyton Manning and zero interceptions to start a season. The streak was ended when he threw an interception against the Detroit Lions in the blizzard game in the second week of December.

Foles finished the 2013 regular season with 27 touchdown passes and only two interceptions which surpassed Tom Brady's 2010 season in which he had 36 touchdown passes and only four interceptions for the best TD-INT ratio in NFL history. He also ended the season leading the NFL in passer rating. Foles's 119.0 passer rating was third in NFL history behind only Aaron Rodgers's 122.5 rating in 2011 and Peyton Manning's 121.1 rating in 2004.

The Eagles had a 10 – 6 record, fueled by a five-game win streak under Foles. They became NFC East Champions and earned their first playoff berth since 2010. The New Orleans Saints traveled to Lincoln Financial Field and handed the Eagles a loss in the playoffs. Foles threw for 195 yards, two touchdowns, and no interceptions but lost due to a last-minute field goal as the game ended at 26–24.

Foles was selected as a Pro Bowl alternate in 2013 and took part in the game after being selected in an All-Star player draft by Team Sanders which was coached by Hall of Fame cornerback Deion Sanders. Team Sanders lost to Team Rice, but Foles was good on seven of his 10 pass attempts for 89 yards and a touchdown. He was named the Offensive MVP of the game.

Foles set an example of being ready when called upon and taking advantage of any opportunities that arise. He started the season as a backup but didn't sulk. Rather he continued to prepare as if he was the starter which resulted in one of the most efficient single seasons by a quarterback in league history.

After such a historic season for Foles, the Eagles were faced with the possibility of having to make a huge financial investment in their young quarterback in a couple of years. Foles needed to show that his 2013 performance was more than just a hot streak.

DeSean Jackson was one of Foles's Super Bowl top targets in 2013. He caught 82 passes for 1,332 yards and scored nine touchdowns as receiver working with Foles and Vick combined. That was not enough to keep Chip Kelly from releasing Jackson in a controversial move before the 2014 season started. Kelly selected former Vanderbilt wideout Jordan Matthews in the second round of the 2014 NFL Draft to help the offense. Darren Sproles was also acquired to provide some scoring power in exchange for a 2014 fifth-round draft pick. Jeremy Maclin was also returning to the lineup after suffering a torn ACL in 2013. Kelly and the Eagles felt they had enough to make up for the loss of Jackson.

Things got off to a rocky start for Foles in 2014. He matched his 2013 season total when he threw two interceptions in the season opener against the Jacksonville Jaguars. Philadelphia fell to an early 17 − 0 deficit, but got things rolling and the team scored 34 unanswered points to win by a score of 34 − 17. Foles completed 24 of 45 passes for 332 yards and two touchdowns but had two interceptions as well.

Foles led the Eagles to a 30 − 27 win over the Colts the following week. He went 21 − 37, passing for 331 yards with a touchdown but also threw another interception. In two weeks, Foles had thrown more interceptions than he did in 13 games in 2013.

In Week Eight, Foles set a franchise record for most completions in a game with 36 which came on a career-high 62 pass attempts against the Arizona Cardinals. The Eagles won the game and Foles had 411 passing yards along with two touchdowns.

Foles's season ended abruptly in Week Nine against the Houston Texans when he left the game with a broken collarbone in the first half. Before exiting the game, Foles completed 9 of his 12 pass attempts for 124 yards. He threw one touchdown pass and an interception as well. The broken collarbone landed Foles on injured reserve and ended his season.

Mark Sanchez came in to replace Foles for the remainder of the season. Sanchez finished the season with 14 touchdown passes and 11 interceptions in eight games. By comparison, Foles was accountable for 13 touchdown passes and 11 interceptions.

The 2015 season was going to be a year in which Foles could cement himself as the quarterback that should lead the Eagles. However, Philadelphia reportedly was not in favor of making a long-term commitment to Foles before the injury ended his season.

"I think Howie is looking at quarterbacks," a source told NJ Advance Media. "He's kind of soured on Foles, and I don't think he's alone. The organization isn't sold that he's the guy going forward. Let's just say the way things were going, he wasn't going to get a contract extension that's for sure."

It was unimaginable that Foles would go from a record-setting quarterback just one season ago to one that struggled in 2014. NFL officially stands for National Football League, but can also stand for Not For Long given how quickly things can change. The league is a bottom-line business, working on a 'What have you done for me lately' basis. That was precisely the case when the Eagles and Rams swapped quarterbacks in an effort to reboot their franchises.

Having gone through the ordeal in St. Louis playing for head coach Jeff Fischer and being rejuvenated in Kansas City with Andy Reid, a return to Philadelphia was perfect for Foles in 2017. He played his part as the backup to Carson Wentz, helping the second-year quarterback prepare each week. When Wentz went down, Foles had to work his way back into form over three games to get ready for the playoffs.

"I sat him down and made him list things he did well with our coaching staff, 'What are your best concepts? What do you see yourself do well?

Because . . . myself, Frank Reich, Doug Pederson—we're not the ones out there throwing it. He is," former QB coach John DeFilippo explained on ESPN.com as he reflected on his time with Foles.

The Eagles coaching staff wanted Foles to 'be himself' and play his game. They were going to run the ball but wanted to give Foles a chance to make plays in the passing game. Foles knew he was capable of leading the team in the playoffs. "I know I can still go out there. I know what I can do. Sports are crazy at times," Foles said after the Eagles lost 6 – 0 to the Cowboys in the regular-season finale on December 31. "You don't always play a hundred percent of what you want to do, but you keep trucking along. You keep working and I feel great. I feel really confident. I know the guys are confident in me."

It was in the playoffs that Foles really started to blossom. The Eagles hadn't been to the postseason since Foles last started for them against the Saints in 2013. This time, another high-powered NFC South offense that played in a dome was coming to Lincoln Financial Field.

"Not trying to force anything but being aggressive. He's an aggressive— he's got an aggressive mindset. I remember his first day here talking to him about how he plays the game and just picking his brain, just talking quarterback play," offensive coordinator Frank Reich said during his weekly press conference when asked about Foles going against the Falcons. "And I could just see his eyes light up with this aggressive mindset: 'I like to throw the ball down the field. I'm an aggressive—I play an aggressive style of ball.' So to be more specific to your question, I think that would be one example."

Head Coach Doug Pederson's message to Foles was to 'go be Nick and execute the offense.' Although Foles hadn't been playing his best football up to that point, Pederson had no doubt that Foles wasn't lacking confidence and was going to be up for the challenge.

"He's handled it great. He's the type of guy, like most quarterbacks, we learn to compartmentalize everything and put things in boxes and just sort of check off each box every day and make sure we're staying focused on the game plan and the guys. He's done a nice job and handled it well this week," Pederson said a few days before the Falcons game.

Pederson dialed up 30 passing plays for Foles against the Falcons. When it mattered the most, Foles led the Eagles on two long drives that resulted in two field goals by Jake Elliott giving them the lead late in the fourth quarter.

The first drive started at Philadelphia's seven-yard line. The Eagles went 74 yards in 12 plays. Most of the yards came on three passes by Foles to Alshon Jeffery that covered a total of 46 yards. Foles also completed passes to tight end Zach Ertz (11 yards) and Torrey Smith (13 yards) on the drive before giving way to Elliott to kick a 37-yard field goal.

After forcing the Falcons to punt, Foles and the offense took over at their own 17-yard line. The Eagles drove the ball down the field with the bulk of the yards coming on a screen pass from Foles to Jay Ajayi that covered 32 yards. The drive ended with a 21-yard field goal by Elliott, giving the Eagles a 15-10 lead.

Foles was clutch for Philadelphia when it mattered the most. Like he did in 2013, Foles handed the defense an opportunity to protect a late lead. The defense held up in dramatic fashion as cornerback Jalen Mills broke up a Matt Ryan pass intended for Julio Jones from two yards out of the end zone.

The Eagles were now headed to the NFC Championship Game. It was going to be played in their backyard. Foles shared a lesson he learned from the Falcons game and the week leading up to it. "You know, I am very humbled to win this game and to be a part of this team. That's what it's always been about. I know there was a lot of people against us this last week," Foles said after the game. "Just answering questions, and just hearing about it. But the biggest thing about this is that it's sports, that's part of it. The biggest thing in our locker room is we believe in one another. Everyone believes, and that was shown on display tonight. The city of Philadelphia obviously believes because they were here and loud."

Having delivered the first playoff win since a divisional round playoff victory over the Giants in 2008, Foles could have puffed his chest out in and told his doubters to look at him now. But that's not in Foles's demeanor. "Because it doesn't matter. They are doing their job, but it doesn't affect how I play or what I believe," Foles said after the game. "And ya'll asked me last week am I confident in myself; well, I am confident in myself because I know how hard we work, and I know that we believe in one another in that locker room. So there is no need to waste my time to say anything about it because we went out there and played great team football. We played Philadelphia Eagle football tonight and that's the most important thing. I don't need to say anything else to anyone."

Even though the Eagles won the game, there was still a degree of doubt in Foles's ability to pass the ball down the field. Ironically, that has been something that was one of his strengths throughout his career. Foles didn't deliver a bunch of deep completions or pass attempts against the Falcons because it wasn't in the game plan. The swirling winds were also a factor. One of Foles's early throws got caught in the wind and resembled a punt.

Frank Reich explained how the game plan was more set up to get the ball in the receiver's hands and let them make plays. "Every game's new. We talked about that, as well, today. That was one of the things that I think we excelled at was the run after catch. That point was made to our players today," Reich said. "Just the aggressiveness with the ball in their hand, protecting the ball, but that is always going to change week-to-week depending on coverages that are being played, depending on the flow of the game. Every week we have a variety of quick, short-, medium-range passes in the game plan. We also have multiple ways to get the ball down the field, and we just kind of feel that out as we go."

Foles would show just how dangerous he could be when he took his shots the following week against the Minnesota Vikings. Going against the Vikings pitted Foles against his former Rams teammate Case Keenum. The two were both starters when they were together in St. Louis in 2015. Now they were starters for opposing teams in the NFC Championship.

"It's pretty wild, absolutely. We were on the same team not too many years ago. I've said over and over again, Case's success and the way he plays doesn't surprise me because he and I were together and we prepared together," Foles said before facing his former teammate. "We were around each other every day. But I think the big message there is no matter what happens, you've just got to keep believing in yourself, keep working hard and just never give up."

Foles looked back on the tough time in St. Louis and how he got through the moments that followed his release from the Rams. It nearly drove him to retire. He got emotional as he talked about his family.

> We're professional athletes and we have moments where we step back and we have to think and assess everything in life. Like I have a family, I have a wife, I have a daughter, I have a dog.
>
> I have to step back and focus on that because that's so important to me. I'm so fortunate that I have my wife there to talk these things through and in these moments where we're playing for this Championship Game, like you do reflect. A few days ago, you just sit there, and I sat there with my wife and we just talked about how blessed we are to be in this moment.

But I know where my heart is and my heart was all being in Philly, being with these guys, going out there on the field, like stepping in the huddle and knowing that each guy is playing for each other, that's a special thing and that's been the testament of this season. And you know it's an honor and blessing to be here and play in this game.

The Eagles had a good week of preparation leading up to the Vikings game. Foles had an even more confident, but laid-back vibe during the week according to Doug Pederson. After calling for a more timing-oriented passing game against the Falcons, Pederson called plays encouraging Foles to push the ball down the field. This style of playcalling was more fitting for the aggressive nature that Foles has when he lines up under center.

The Vikings were bringing the top-ranked defense in the NFL to Lincoln Financial Field. Led by defensive end Everson Griffin, Minnesota had a plan for how to shut down the Eagles. "We've got to make Nick Foles win the game. Affect him and give the ball back to our offense as much as possible so they can score points," Griffen said during his press conference a few days before the game. "The biggest thing with Nick Foles is you've got to get around him. You've got to affect him and make him be a little hesitant in the pocket. With no pressure, he has a very good passer rating, but when he's getting hit, it comes down a lot. We have to get to him in different ways, but we have to stop the run first to get to him."

Foles and the Eagles offense shredded Minnesota's defense. One of Foles's best plays came when a defender got pressure on him and he stepped up in the pocket before delivering a strike down the field to Alshon Jeffery for a 53-yard touchdown.

"It was sort of a broken play where they thought they probably had a sack. I was able to get out and Alshon [Jeffrey] made an amazing play. He saw the coverage and he sort of approached it like a scramble drill," Foles said of the touchdown pass after the game. "I was able to get away and get the ball out there to him, and he made a great catch. The offensive line did a great job blocking all night first and foremost."

"I saw him in the pocket like he was moving around a little bit, but I saw him look backside. He looked at me, but when I looked and turned in, I was hoping he didn't throw it," said Jeffrey. "When I saw him move, I thought it was a scramble play and I just took it up field and he did a great job of finding me," Jeffery said regarding the play.

Player Spotlight: Nick Foles

Even though the Eagles had a 24-7 lead coming out of halftime, Pederson was still aggressive as he dialed up a flea-flicker that led to a 42-yard touchdown on a perfect pass from Foles to Torrey Smith. By the time the game was over, Foles had completed 26 of 33 for 352 yards and three touchdowns and the Eagles' 38 – 7 win punched their ticket to Super Bowl LII.

"My hat's off to Nick. Trusting in his ability, trusting in me as the head coach and putting him in ideal situations and situations to be successful on the field. Then for the guys. The guys to believe in him," Pederson said after the game. "Listen, he's not a rookie. He's a veteran player who has played a lot of games in this league. He's started a lot of games. He had a Pro Bowl year a couple years ago. So this is not a rookie we're talking about. Just so happy for him and what he's been through and everything now to finally put not only himself but help this football team get to where we want to go and hopefully finish the year right."

Foles admitted to wanting to be aggressive against the Vikings. He wanted to attack them and bring the fight to their defense. That's exactly what they did and now they were headed to the Super Bowl. The Eagles worked to keep everything in perspective and not let the added pressure of going against New England's mystique weigh them down in the Super Bowl.

One of the things that helped Foles was his faith. It was his faith that led him back to football in the first place. "It took a lot more faith to go back and play than if it would have gone the other direction. I'm grateful to have this opportunity to speak, to play in this game, but at the same time, if I would've made the other decision, my life wouldn't have been a loss. I would have done something else and glorified God in that instance," Foles said.

"The reason I decided to come back is I loved the game of football since I was a kid. I loved playing sports, loved being part of a team. I knew as a person the more growth I would have, the more opportunity to glorify God and trust in Him so I was able to go back and play football because of everything I had encountered."

Going against a legendary quarterback like Tom Brady is blown completely out of proportion in the Super Bowl. There was this mythical presence being placed on Brady and the Patriots. "To beat them we have to do what we do and that's play great team ball. All year long we have leaned on each other. If you look at the sideline during the game, everyone is getting excited. We all have each other's back. Yeah, beating Tom [Brady], beating the Patriots, is huge, but for me, it's about the journey and the men that I have done it with," Foles said on opening media night in Minnesota.

To beat the Patriots, the Eagles had to play the game of their lives. Just before the first half was over, Foles and the Eagles offense executed a play that will go down as one of the most significant plays in Philadelphia sports history. During a timeout just before the Eagles were facing a fourth and goal, Foles came to the sideline to talk to Pederson. Foles suggested running a play that is now known as the 'Philly Special.'

"How about Philly, Philly?" Foles said.

Pederson looked at Foles as he thought about the play.

"Yeah, let's do it!" Pederson uttered back.

Foles went to the huddle and called the play to the delight of everyone around him. It worked to perfection as Foles became the first quarterback to catch a touchdown pass and throw a touchdown pass in the Super Bowl.

"That's something we've been working on, and Doug [Pederson] and I were talking. I was like, 'Let's just run it.' It was a good time, and the end was a little wider than I thought, so I was like, 'I really need to sell like I'm not doing anything.' And it worked. Trey [Burton] made an amazing throw, right on the money. I just looked it in, and yeah, we've repped it for a while, so I was excited to get it run in the Super Bowl," Foles said as he described the play after the game. The play gave the Eagles a 22 – 12 lead at halftime.

The 'Philly Special' wasn't the only spectacular play for Foles and the Eagles. Foles's ball placement was nearly perfect on two other touchdown throws. He delivered a perfect drop shot right over the shoulder and into the hands of running back Corey Clement for a 22-yard touchdown.

Foles also hit Zach Ertz in stride on a slant that went for a touchdown to give Philadelphia the lead for good. After giving the defense the lead, Foles told defensive captain Malcolm Jenkins to go win the game when he got to the sideline. That's exactly what they did as they forced Brady to fumble the ball on one series and clung to the lead as a Hail Mary pass intended for tight end Rob Gronkowski fell incomplete as the final seconds expired from the clock.

The Eagles had done the unthinkable. Foles was brilliant, completing 28 of 43 pass attempts for 373 yards, three passing touchdowns, and an interception. He was named the MVP of Super Bowl LII.

Player Spotlight: Nick Foles

Foles was even more outstanding when he revealed another lesson from his football experience. Every year there are stories about players who are able to conquer less than ideal circumstances and excel at the highest level. It is great to focus on the good things that happen, but growing through failure makes success all the more cherishable. Foles's story teaches the importance of continuing to fight despite failure.

"The big thing is don't be afraid to fail. In our society today with Instagram and Twitter, it's all highlight reel," Foles said during his Super Bowl LII MVP press conference on Monday. "All of the good things, but when you look at it and failure is a part of life. That's a part of building character and growing. Without failure, who would you be? I wouldn't be up here if I hadn't fallen thousands of times and made mistakes."

"I am not perfect, I am not Superman. I may be in the NFL and we just won the Super Bowl, but I still have daily struggles," Foles explained. "When you look at struggles in life, know that it's an opportunity to grow. If something is going wrong in life, embrace it because you're growing."

Foles was right. His story taught a lot of lessons, but the biggest one was to always be ready because there is no telling when another opportunity will arise and to embrace tough times because it is the fiber of a person's character.

The Philadelphia sports scene had embraced their share of tough times. They went through over five decades of having never won a Super Bowl. Being able to celebrate the city's first Lombardi Trophy was the reward.

"To be a part of the Philadelphia Eagles first championship, we've all waited a long time to be in this position, to be world champions. The people who bleed green, the people of Philadelphia, the people all across the nation that support the Eagles, they've waited a long time. Mr. [Jeffrey] Lurie has waited a long time. Being a part of this, being drafted to Philadelphia, being fortunate enough to come back and be a part of this team, to be a piece of this puzzle, it has been a long time coming," Foles said from the podium after the Super Bowl.

How long Foles was going to be able to be a piece of the puzzle came into question right away. As a Super Bowl MVP, one would think it would be hard for Foles to step back into the backup role when Carson Wentz returned from injury to take over as the starter. Foles wasn't immune to that. He admitted he'd like to lead a team again, but also said he's grateful to be a part of the Eagles.

How much Foles was at peace despite multiple possible outcomes taught yet another lesson, to live in the moment. "There are times when I am tempted to look into the future. I'd be lying if I said that wasn't the case, but you have to reel back in and focus on the present because that doesn't give you any benefit," Foles said.

There were a lot of trade reports floating around about Foles during the offseason. He ended up staying in Philadelphia and signed a contract extension that would reward him depending on how much he played. It was the right situation for Foles. He gets to stay in Philadelphia another year and be a part of a team that he loves.

"The grass isn't always greener on the other side. We have a great team here, we have a great coaching staff. Right now I am going to be the best teammate that I can be. There is so much here that I really enjoy. I love it here," Foles said.

Appendix A

<u>Doug Pederson Unplugged</u>

On Challenges of Being a Head Coach:

The biggest challenge was getting your own study time in. A lot of the other things that you have to do as far as leading the football team, meeting with doctors, meeting with Howie Roseman and the personnel department, meeting with the president, meeting with the owner. Those kinds of things can take away your time during the week. It's about finding time to get your own study and preparation in and being in a position to help your team.

On Being Underestimated:

As a player, I was a career backup. That was my role, and I embraced that role. I had a chance to start, but ultimately my place was to be the backup and support the starter.

As a coach, I am sure there was doubt. There was skepticism. Call it whatever it is. 'First-time head coach, what does he know about running a team?' Hopefully, I have proven people wrong. It was fair, but it didn't motivate me. I was confident in my ability. I was confident in things that I know and the mentoring that I received along the way. I just had to lean on those experiences.

I am motivated to win. I want to win games. That's why we get in this business. That's the motivation. I want to see these guys succeed on the field. I want to teach. When they score touchdowns or pick off passes—sack the quarterback—that is part of teaching. That's the fun part of it.

At the end of the day, you have to have players. This league is about players. Put ninety-eight percent talent in the room and put two percent coaching, but the coaching has to be one hundred percent of the two percent.

I know what's going on here. You are seeing the fundamentals and techniques of what these coaches are teaching the players, then you are seeing it executed during games. That's what you want. That gives our players with talent greater success during these games.

On Philadelphia:

I spent a couple of years here as a player. I came back and coached for four. It's been a great place for me and my family. There's a part of me that—this underdog mentality, 'you can't do something' mentality—I think is kind of the city of Philly.

They say you can't do something and next thing you know you rise up and do something amazing. That's kind of who I am. I have always been one of those jack of all trade athletes. Good at everything but master of none. That's been my career. To come back to a city that embraces that role, to rise up and lead a group of guys that had a lot of adversity thrown in their face, that's kind of what draws you to this.

I understand the culture and passion of Philadelphia. I experienced it firsthand. I understand what it feels like to win in this city. This city, this organization hasn't won in quite some time. It's my job to turn that around.

On Don Shula, Mike Holmgren, and Andy Reid and His Evolution:

I think the longer a person is somewhere, the team starts taking on the personality of the coach a little bit. You start hearing the same thing come from their mouths that I was saying in here. They start believing. You are starting to see on the field—run, play action—the things that I believe in. I think we are a good football team doing those things. Staying sound in those areas. The physicality with the defensive line. That's where you start. As a team, they start taking on your personality. That's what you want as a head coach.

On QB Room:

There is a lot of ball being talked in that room. The three guys break down a lot of tape. When Nick started, it stayed the same. Carson took the role of Nick and helped with breaking down the tape. You get a lot of conversations coming out of that room. I go in there every day. I am not in their morning meetings but when we are watching tape, I want to make sure they feel my presence, and they can ask questions they may have.

I can remember the same types of meetings that went on with Brett and Steve Bono and myself or with Jim McMahon. We probably did a lot more studying on our own than we did as a group but there was still the conversations that we have with our coach and the coordinator at the time.

Appendix B

<u>What They Are Saying</u>

Andy Reid on Doug Pederson's Rapid Ascension to Head Coach:

"He got in and loved every minute of it," Reid said Monday of Pederson, who took just five years to advance from quality control coach to head coach.

"He gobbled it up, and he earned every position that he got. I don't think people who had worked with him were surprised he had the opportunity to be a coordinator, and then I don't think they were surprised when he had the opportunity to be a head coach.

"The guys who worked with him knew what he was capable of doing, and so what seemed like a fast-paced progression for people outside of here seemed kind of natural for the people who were here. I have a lot of respect for him, and I think he's doing a nice job there."

Mike Sherman on Doug Pederson:

"Doug was a student of the game even back then," Sherman told the Canadian Press National Post before the Super Bowl. "Did I think he'd be a Super Bowl coach in his second season? No. But I knew he'd be a heck of a coach. I'm not surprised that he's here, but it definitely happened faster than I expected."

Pederson has credited both Sherman and Mike Holmgren as influential figures when it comes to playcalling.

"He's giving me way too much credit for that. He's developed his own pattern of play calling. But he was with us for five years. We did a bunch of different things that he was privy to. He was a smart guy back then and probably grabbed onto the things that worked and got rid of the things that didn't work. But Doug Pederson is where he is because of who he is, and he'd be there with or without me, I'm sure about that."

Mike Sherman on Favre's Trust in Pederson:

"Doug had great vision of the field and was able to communicate that to the coaches and players. So he was coaching the whole time he was the backup to Brett Favre. This is not something he's just stumbled upon. He's been a coach since I've known him because of how he took his role as backup quarterback."

Brett Favre on Doug Pederson Coaching:

"I can't say that I knew he would coach, but I knew that if he did coach, he had something in him," Favre told NFL Network's game day special before Super Bowl LII. "You just know."

"I was kind of surprised when he decided to go into coaching, but I'm not surprised he's had the success he's had, and he's moved up this quickly,"

Mike Holmgren on Doug Pederson

"As the backup quarterback, not the starter, you're learning a lot, you're thinking a lot, you're watching the coach and what he does, and Doug was a very serious student that way," Holmgren told Jeff McLane of Philly. com.

"And he had a great personality and all that stuff fit. Doug would have that kind of influence and Brett would have that kind respect for him. That made sense because Brett can be off the cuff sometimes and Doug was a little more by the numbers."

About the Author

NFL reporter **Turron Davenport** has provided credentialed coverage of the San Francisco 49ers in addition to serving as a beat writer covering the Baltimore Ravens, Philadelphia Eagles, and currently the Tennessee Titans. Davenport is a member of the Pro Football Writers Association. He is currently the ESPN's NFL Nation Titans reporter.

Davenport worked as an NFL Draft Analyst for Footballgameplan.com and co-authored a two-part book series called *Football: A Love Story and What Did Football Teach Me?* His is also the author of *Carson Wentz: Soaring with the Eagles.* Davenport has provided live coverage of NFL events including multiple Super Bowls, Reese's Senior Bowl, East-West Shrine Game, NFL Draft, and the NFL Combine.